# Music Library Association Technical Reports Series

Edited by Philip Vandermeer

# Guide to Writing Collection Development Policies for Music

Amanda Maple
Jean Morrow

indexed by Kristina L. Shanton

*Music Library Association
Technical Reports, No. 26*

The Scarecrow Press, Inc.
Lanham, Maryland, and London
and
Music Library Association
2001

# SCARECROW PRESS, INC.

Published in the United States of America
by Scarecrow Press, Inc.
4720 Boston Way, Lanham, Maryland 20706
www.scarecrowpress.com

4 Pleydell Gardens, Folkestone
Kent CT20 2DN, England

British Library Cataloguing in Publication Information Available

**Library of Congress Cataloging-in-Publication Data**

Maple, Amanda, 1956–
    Guide to writing collection development policies for music / Amanda Maple,
    Jean Morrow.
       p. cm. — (Music Library Association technical reports ; no. 26)
    Includes bibliographical references and index.
    ISBN 0-8108-4006-5 (alk. paper) — ISBN 0-8108-3865-6 (pbk. : alk. paper)
      1. Music libraries—Collection development—United States—Policy
    statements. 2. Collection development—United States—Policy statements. 3.
    Music librarianship—United States. I. Morrow, Jean, 1944– II. Title. III. MLA
    technical reports ; no. 26.
    ML111.M36 2001
    025.2'88—dc21                                    00-067938

# Contents

# Preface

The need for this guide was identified by the Resource Sharing and Collection Development Committee, Music Library Association. Its format is adapted in part from the American Library Association's *Guide for Written Collection Policy Statements* (1996) and *Reference Collection Development: A Manual* (1992). We relied on sources cited in the notes as well as on unpublished work done by members of the Resource Sharing and Collection Development Committee to outline issues involved in the development of music collections in libraries. We gratefully acknowledge the careful reading of various versions of this text and the helpful comments and suggestions from our fellow members of the Resource Sharing and Collection Development Committee: Brad Short, chair, 1995–1997; William Coscarelli, chair, 1997– ; Elizabeth Davis, David Day, John Druesedow, Mark Germer, and Janet Winzenburger. We also thank Dan Cherubin and Barbara Sutherland for reading and commenting on the text, and especially acknowledge William E. Anderson for his extensive comments and suggestions.

We wish to thank the following institutions and librarians for permission to include excerpts from their collection policies:

> Bowling Green State University, Sound Recordings Archives; William Schurk, Sound Recordings Archivist
> Columbus Metropolitan Library, Main Library
> Duke University, Music Library; John E. Druesedow Jr., Director
> Middlebury College, Music Library; Jerry McBride, Music Librarian
> New York University, Bobst Library; Kent Underwood, Music Librarian

North Carolina School of the Arts, Semans Library; Vicki L. Montle, Library Director, and Leslie Kamtman, Music Librarian

St. Olaf College, Halvorson Music Library; Beth Christensen, Music Librarian

University of California at Los Angeles, Music Library; Stephen M. Fry, Music Librarian

University of Hartford, The Hartt School, Allen Library; Linda Solow Blotner, Head Librarian

University of Illinois at Urbana-Champaign, Music Library; Richard Griscom, Music Librarian

University of Iowa, Rita Benton Music Library; Joan O. Falconer, Music Librarian

University of Western Ontario, Music Library; Sister Louise Smith and Jane A. Pearce Baldwin

Amanda Maple
Pennsylvania State University

Jean Morrow
New England Conservatory of Music

# Introduction

This guide is intended to assist librarians, both music specialists and generalists, who are responsible for writing collection development policies for music collections in academic, conservatory, and public libraries. It is meant to supplement the American Library Association's *Guide for Written Collection Policy Statements*,[1] and writers of collection policies for music are strongly encouraged to consult that publication. Every music collection is unique and all of the points addressed in this guide do not apply to all music collections. Readers are urged to make use of those sections relevant to their particular situations.

The checklist in chapter 1 delineates the sections that might be included in a collection development policy for music and discusses issues specific to the selection of various formats of music materials. The outline of a sample policy in chapter 2 contains examples from actual collection development policies for music. Chapter 3 consists of a complete collection development policy from the Middlebury College Music Library written by Jerry McBride. The appendix gives instructions for obtaining copies of the collection development policies for music on file with the chair of the Resource Sharing and Collection Development Committee of the Music Library Association. A glossary and selected bibliography conclude this guide.

Collection development policies are fundamentally planning documents. The forward-looking process of collection development is a continuous response to the changing needs of the dynamic institutions and user groups associated with libraries. According to the *Guide for Written Collection Policy Statements*, collection development is "the process of planning, building and maintaining a library's information resources in a cost-effective and user-relevant manner."[2] In addition to identification and selection of locally appropriate materials, the collection development process includes liaison work with users, planning, and implementing resource sharing programs, and *collection management* activities: "collection analysis and evaluation; collection review for decision making on preservation, protected access, remote storage, or discard; use and user studies; vendor and dealer assessments; and other methods of study and measurement."[3] Therefore, the library's policies for preservation and for review of the collection for relocation or deselection should be incorporated into or coordinated with the collection development policy, since these activities are part of the collection development process.[4] Any collection development policy for music should take into consideration other policies in force at the institution, including other collection development policies and collection management policies for preservation, deselection, access, interlibrary loan, and consortial agreements. The music collection development policy should not contradict other institutional policies.

The need for written collection development policies has been questioned within the profession of librarianship. Collection development policies can be inflexibly written; can quickly become out of date; can be used to defend arbitrarily the status quo when librarians are asked to support new programs or users. New trends in the creation and dissemination of information may not fit neatly into the subject and format categories traditionally contained in collection development policies.[5] Writing a policy involves evaluation of the collection, which is difficult and time consuming (and therefore expensive). And the claim that written policies promote resource sharing among libraries has been challenged.[6] Richard Snow suggests that devising an effective approval plan involves the same process as writing a collection development policy, but has practical benefits (for example, the addition of library materials to the collection) that a collection development policy lacks. Rather than writing a collection development policy, he says, "a better use of the bibliographer's time would be an evaluation of how material in the library is used, and why."[7]

We agree that collection development policies should not be used as an excuse to avoid serving the needs of changing user groups, and that policies should be written flexibly and updated frequently. A well-written collection policy "clearly describes an individual library's objectives in developing its collections and in providing access to off-site information through electronic means or document delivery."[8] The focus of collection development policies need not be limited to print materials, but should consider all formats acquired by the library. The variety of information formats acquired for most music collections requires transactions with many vendors and publishers, thus diminishing the argument to substitute an approval plan for a written collection development policy for music. Policies should also address information not acquired locally but rather made accessible to library users from remote locations. "Flexible descriptions that encompass all formats of information and resources both local and remote will require continuous adjustment as each field's methods and materials evolve. Libraries will therefore have to focus continuously on users' priorities and needs. Strategies for hard copy acquisitions will follow and derive from these general analyses."[9] No library can afford to collect all published information, nor would many libraries want to, regardless of content, even if they could. Therefore, library selectors make decisions about what to collect and not collect. Whether or not they use written collection policies, all selectors base their decisions on some criteria. Library selectors are responsible for deciding which information sources to provide for their users and how best to provide them: acquiring them for the library's shelves; document delivery systems; electronic access; or resource sharing with other institutions.[10]

The *Guide for Written Collection Policy Statements* delineates several uses for written collection policies.[11] If the policy is intended to be a document for public distribution in addition to being a working document for the music selector, it is necessary to keep in mind the possibility that such a document could become politicized. A flexibly written policy will serve collection development needs better than one written in so much detail that it easily becomes outdated. Whatever the intended use of the policy, the *process* of writing and regularly revising it, of asking and answering the kinds of questions outlined in this guide (such as reviewing the mission of the specific library, identifying user groups, perusing the course bulletin in an academic library and looking at the courses offered across campus) can be of great benefit to the writer of the policy. The resulting document also assists newly hired music selectors and interim selectors. In addition, it helps reference librarians and selectors in other subject areas in the institution to understand the scope of the music collection and the criteria for its selection. Collection development policies also promote communication between selectors and administrators in other libraries within a consortium and other institutions.[12]

This guide will serve as a practical aid to music selectors writing or revising collection policies in the ongoing effort to meet their goals for the collections under their care and to address the needs of the users of those collections.

# 1

# Checklist for Writing a Collection Development Policy for Music

A collection development policy for music generally includes the following three sections:

    I.    Introduction

    II.    Summary of the scope of coverage at current collecting levels (including a discussion of formats collected)

    III.    Detailed analysis of the collection

This suggested organization is not prescriptive; some writers of collection policies for music choose to move certain elements from the introduction to a later section, for example, or to conflate sections II and III. These three sections are presented in the following pages, along with issues to be considered when selecting music.

Included are only those sections or points that pertain to the specific collection and institution under consideration. Not all items will be included in every written collection development policy for music.

## I. Introduction

The introduction might serve some or all of the following functions:[13]

A. State the purpose of the policy.

The *Guide for Written Collection Policy Statements* identifies several purposes for collection development policies.[14] The purpose of the policy is related to its intended audience, and it is useful to consider intended readers when writing this section.

B. Generally describe the institution and define the clientele and programs associated with the collection.

Music collections are housed in various types of libraries (public, academic, or conservatory) and in support of orchestra and opera companies, radio and television shows, recording manufacturers, historical societies, monasteries, seminaries, and so forth. As with all libraries, the development and management of collections in music libraries is based on their specific purposes and user communities. Before writing a collection development policy, the mission of the library, its user groups, and the purposes of the music collection must be identified.

Some libraries have a strong research constituency. If a library's user groups include undergraduate or graduate music majors, levels of students can be delineated. If one of the collection's purposes is to provide printed music for performance, the collection development policy can describe levels such as professional, amateur, beginner, undergraduate, or graduate. In academic libraries, relevant curricula and academic programs can be identified (e.g., musicology, ethnomusicology, performance, music education, music pedagogy, composition, music technology, theater studies, film studies, dance, popular culture studies, communication, etc.) and the level of each program can be specified. Other purposes of music collections include the facilitation of recreation and community enrichment. The act of writing a collection development policy encourages the writer to learn about the institution, the users, and the collection. In *Developing Public Library Collections, Policies, and Procedures,* Kay Ann Cassell and Elizabeth Futas describe methods public librarians can use to identify the needs and interests of their user community, including patron surveys and community support groups.[15]

Libraries are places where teaching and learning are facilitated, and where discovery and the imparting of knowledge occur. Both public and academic libraries supplement and amplify teaching and learning that originates in classrooms and, moreover, provide the means to challenge or transform the classroom experience. The points of departure for collection policies are the institutional mission and, in academic libraries, the curricula of the constituent departments. However, the synthesis of these is more than the sum of the parts. In this context, collection development becomes a library-focused process of shaping a body of representative information sources rather than an externally focused process of random buying in support of current programs.

C. State the mission and goals of the collection management and development program.

Policies for music collections that are part of a larger institutional library system can incorporate or refer to statements of the library system's mission and goals for the collection program. Music collection policies also frequently incorporate this section into the previous section B in the description of the clientele and programs related to the collection.

D. Include or refer to the institutional library system's official statements about intellectual freedom, censorship, and copyright issues.

E. Provide a brief overview of the collection, including prominent features of its history if appropriate, and the location(s) of its holdings (including remote storage).

F. Identify persons responsible for building and maintaining the collection.

In addition to stating the position(s) with responsibility for collection management and development, include a summary of liaison or advisory relationships if appropriate. For example, the music selector in an academic library may meet regularly with music faculty, or perhaps with a formal faculty library committee, to solicit input about developing the music collections. Public libraries with more than one branch may designate a subject specialist at the main branch to be responsible for music selection at all branches, or branch librarians may be responsible for music selection at their own branches. This responsibility can be shared, with the subject specialist providing suggestions to the branch librarians in the form of selection lists.

G. Outline the relationship of the collection development policy to collection management programs for preservation, storage, replacement, deselection, and access (including the procurement of equipment and technical support for the provision of access).

Policies regarding these collection management activities should be incorporated into or coordinated with the collection development policy. Reviewing materials in the collection for retention, preservation, relocation, or deselection is as important to the maintenance of collections as selecting new materials. Writers of collection development policies for music are strongly encouraged to consult resources such as the *Guide to the Evaluation of Library Collections* and the *Guide to Review of Library Collections: Preservation, Storage, and Withdrawal*.[16] Music materials can be particularly problematic to house and preserve. For example, performance parts and sheet music require special arrangements for shelving, such as custom binding or archival boxing. Deselection policies for music may be different from those for other material formats and disciplines of study. Timeliness may be excluded as a deselection factor for music, since older performing editions and recordings contain evidence of earlier performance practices.

Access to information, as distinguished from ownership of information, is a critical collection development issue and should be addressed in the collection development policy. Providing access electronically to remote information sources is one example of access rather than ownership; see the discussion of electronic formats in section II.B.4. In addition, incorporate or refer to policies regarding technical support and the purchase of equipment for onsite and remote electronic files and texts. Information that requires equipment for access, such as electronic information requiring computer hardware or audio and visual information requiring playback equipment, becomes unavailable to users when the equipment needed for access becomes outdated and is not maintained. Incorporate or refer to policies guiding decisions about the transfer of such information to an accessible format or for continued maintenance of the equipment.

H. Describe cooperative collecting agreements and consortial agreements (including interlibrary loan).

The sharing of resources among institutions through inter-library loan and cooperative collecting are other examples of providing access to information; policies regarding these pro-grams should be noted in the collection development policy.

I. Delineate procedures and a timeline for regular review and revision of the collection development policy.

## II. Summary of the scope of coverage at current collecting levels

A. Broad categories of music

Types of music that may be collected or excluded include western art; jazz; popular; and ethnic, folk, or world. Indicate whether these categories are collected at the same or varying levels.

B. Formats
  1. Books and other textual materials
     Types of materials collected can include reference works, periodicals, monographs (including dissertations), librettos, and publishers' and dealers' catalogs.

  2. Printed music
     Printed music exists in various physical formats, some of which are intended for performance and others for study. Formats include full scores, condensed scores, miniature scores or study scores, close scores, vocal scores, chorus scores, piano scores, and parts. Indicate formats that are systematically collected or excluded. (Further discussion of the types of printed music collected in libraries is found at III.B.1.h: Editions collected or excluded.)

  3. Recordings
     Various disk and tape formats for sound recordings (e.g., 78 rpm, 45 rpm, 33 1/3 rpm, compact discs, open reel, cassette) and video recordings (e.g., laser disc, DVD, VHS) are collected by music libraries. Decisions about collecting or excluding various formats are sometimes based on whether playback equipment for a particular format is available to users in the library. Formats for which there is no public playback equipment are excluded in some libraries. Other libraries collect formats for which they have no playback equipment and circulate the materials to patrons for use on equipment located elsewhere. These types of policies can be noted here.

     a. Sound
        Collection issues related to sound recordings that could be noted here, if appropriate, include the collection of more than one performance of the same work. Some libraries purposely acquire several different recorded performances of a work,

including reissues of early recorded performances, to support the study of music performance, reception history, and other aspects of the discipline. Some libraries systematically collect the entire output of one or more publishers ("labels"). Efforts to coordinate the recordings collection with the printed music collection can be noted. Some libraries prefer to select recordings of the composer as performer or conductor rather than other recordings of the same work. Policies regarding the selection of reissues of popular music and jazz can also be noted: for example, preference for "greatest hits" reissues and other types of sampler collections, or preference for "complete works" reissues.

b. Video

The visual component of the performance of dramatic musical works (operas, ballets, etc.) can greatly enhance the study of these works. Other excellent uses of video in the study of music include demonstrations of technique (e.g., how to conduct, how to hold a bow, how to make reeds) and study of the performance environment (e.g., ethnomusicological studies). Recording standards for video differ around the world (NTSC, PAL, and SECAM are defined in the glossary); decisions about recording standards selected or excluded may be based on the availability of playback equipment and can be noted here if applicable.

4. Electronic formats

Electronic formats are those that require computer access. These resources may be mounted locally on a microcomputer or mainframe computer, or may be made available from a remote computer. Access may be provided through a local or wide area network, through the Internet, or from a single workstation only. Physical formats include floppy disks, CD-ROMs, and magnetic tape. Types of sources available include electronic journals, reference works, bibliographic databases, full-text databases, interactive multimedia products, notational software, and computer music. Any collection policies specific to electronic resources can be noted here.

The intellectual content of electronic resources, as with all types of sources, is an important criterion for selection. Multimedia music products, for example, can be especially suitable for educational purposes and could be appropriate for collections with a music education constituency. Institutional policies regarding the signing of license agreements and the provision of local technological support must be considered by selectors. The availability of appropriate computer hardware is an important consideration. For example, does the type of computer hardware locally available influence decisions about which electronic formats are collected? Factors that can influence selectors' decisions about providing local vs. remote access to an electronic resource include hardware and network capabilities, available institutional support, copyright issues, and price. In many institutions it is the music selector's responsibility to identify appropriate music resources on the Internet and take steps to make them readily accessible to the library's users. This responsibility can be seen as a part of collection development and included in the collection development policy for music.

Policies that guide decisions about replacing ownership of printed volumes with electronic access to the information can be incorporated here. The Association of Research Libraries' SPEC Kit 207, *Organization of Collection Development*, contains sample collection development policies for electronic resources.[17]

5. Microforms

The availability of appropriate playback equipment is again a consideration when deciding whether to collect microforms and where in the library to house them. Microforms are one of the standard formats used to preserve deteriorating print materials in libraries. They also save shelf space. Many libraries purchase back issues of periodicals on microfilm, for example.

6. Manuscripts and early editions

Research and scholarship in music often incorporate the study of manuscripts and early editions. A library's acquisition of rare or one-of-a-kind materials brings with it an institutional responsibility to preserve these materials carefully and to strictly supervise their use to ensure that they are available to future generations of scholars. Such materials are often collected in conjunction with a special collection or archives. Criteria for selection may include whether the item supports the research needs of specific local scholars; whether appropriately supervised access is readily available to scholars; whether researchers from other institutions can be made aware of the location of the item and will have access to it; and whether acquisition of the item will enhance existing strengths of the collection. Not all music collections acquire these materials; these collection policies can be noted here.

C. Local or regional artists' or writers' works collected systematically

Summarize policies regarding the collection of music by local performers and composers; writings by local writers and scholars; programs of local performances; etc.

D. Writings about music

Types of writings about music that may be collected or excluded include scholarly (e.g., dissertations; scholarly writings about popular music); professional (e.g., professional journals to support the work of performers); instructional (e.g., curriculum materials for music education; textbooks); and popular (e.g., magazines written for popular audiences; fanzines).

E. Languages

Note inclusions or exclusions based on language. Some libraries exclude writings about music that are in foreign languages. Language exclusions may or may not apply equally to reference works, monographs, and periodicals, or to scholarly and popular writings. ʼ

When collecting vocal music with text, it is the policy in some libraries to collect printed editions and recordings in the original language of the work. In addition, certain translations, such as English, may also be systematically collected. These policies may or may not apply to the collection of librettos. Language of the editorial information accompanying printed editions and recordings may also be considered in a policy.

F. Multiple copies of a single edition

It is policy in some libraries to acquire as many copies of an edition as are required for performance, when more than one copy is required. Policy about acquiring multiple copies for classroom use varies among academic institutions and can be noted here. Some libraries acquire second copies of non-circulating scores to provide circulating copies. Public libraries frequently acquire multiple copies of items in great demand that circulate frequently.

G. Pedagogical materials

Note inclusions or exclusions of pedagogical materials, such as instrumental methods and studies, textbooks, orchestral excerpts, and curriculum materials (school song books, graded instrumental parts with teacher's guides, lesson plan kits, etc.). If appropriate, indicate levels of difficulty or intellectual content collected.

H. Standing orders and approval plans

Describe or refer to any standing orders and approval plans that have an impact on the music collections. For example, some public libraries arrange to have sound recording dealers supply on approval all recordings that reach a certain level of popularity according to one or more charts. Various dealers of printed music, books, and recordings of western art music are also willing to set up approval plans for libraries. Standing orders for particular series of printed music, recordings, and monographs are also common.

I. Selection tools

Some collection policies for music include references to suggested selection tools, such as sources of reviews, specific dealers' and publishers' catalogs, etc. In the chapter on music in *Selection of Library Materials in the Humanities, Social Sciences, and Sciences*,[18] Michael A. Keller discusses the many factors involved in selecting and acquiring all formats of music for research libraries, concentrating on western art music. He concludes with a list of selection sources that are described in the text of his essay: journals that provide reviews and lists of new publications; bibliographies, discographies, and other reference tools; and dealers and their catalogs. At the end of this guide is a selected bibliography of other articles that provide guidance in the selection of various types of music and music information for libraries, and readers are encouraged to survey the professional literature regularly for similar works. In addition, books offering advice about the selection of music materials can be found in library catalogs under subject headings such as "Sound recordings—Collectors and collecting," "Video recordings—Collectors and collecting," "Music—Collectors and collecting," "Compact discs—Reviews," "Audiocassettes—Reviews," "Music—Discography," "Jazz—Discography," "Country Music—Discography," "Blues (Music)—Discography," and so forth.

Bibliographies, discographies, and histories devoted to particular types of music are useful collection assessment tools, enabling a selector to assess the breadth and depth of current holdings before deciding if new or retrospective materials need to be acquired. The bibliographies and discographies in *A Basic Music Library: Essential Scores and Sound Recordings* and the appendix to Elizabeth Davis's "Guidelines for Evaluating Music Collections as Part of a Regional Assessment Plan" are especially useful lists of collection assessment tools.[19] Check for new editions of assessment tools listed in such bibliographies, which quickly become outdated.

J. Gifts

Policies for accepting gifts, if different from criteria for acquiring material by purchase, should be described, including policies about accepting gifts accompanied by restrictions on use, housing, etc.

K. Replacements

Describe any special criteria for decisions regarding the replacement of missing or damaged items.

L. Course reserves

Describe any special criteria for selecting materials for course reserves.

M. Expensive purchases

Describe any special criteria or procedures for the selection of items that cost more than a certain amount.

N. Access and ownership policies

Describe or refer to policies that guide decisions about when to provide access to information (e.g., electronic access or document delivery) rather than purchase a physical copy of the information for the library's shelves.

## III. Detailed analysis of the collection

Two methods for describing the collection in detail are presented in the *Guide for Written Collection Policy Statements*: the conspectus approach and the narrative statement approach.[20]

### *Conspectus approach*

A conspectus is "an overview or summary of collection strengths and collecting intensities—arranged by subject, classification scheme, or a combination of either, and containing standardized codes for collection or collecting levels and for languages of materials collected."[21] Using the conspectus approach to describe collecting levels involves assigning to predetermined subsets of any library classification scheme numeric (or alphanumeric) codes that represent different levels of collecting. In addition to describing current collecting levels, the conspectus approach can include indications of goals for future collecting levels. Articles by Jane Gottlieb, Peggy Daub, and Elizabeth Davis in *Collection Assessment in Music Libraries* describe the use of the conspectus approach in the assessment of music collections.[22] Collection assessment and collection development are distinct activities: assessment involves evaluating materials already in the collection; development addresses current and future needs for the collection and involves selecting materials to best meet those needs. The process of collection development usually involves a basic level of assessment: current holdings are checked before the purchase of new material to avoid redundancy and to assess the need for the new material. Collection assessment tools, such as *A Basic Music Library* and others listed on pages 38–49 of *Collection Assessment in Music Libraries*, are useful for the work of retrospective collection development as well as for collection assessment.

The articles in *Collection Assessment in Music Libraries* will be useful to writers of collection development policies for music who wish to use the conspectus approach to describe their collecting levels. The appendix in *Collection Assessment in Music Libraries* lists the predetermined subsets of music subject categories in the *Library of Congress Classification* (*LCC*) used by the Research Libraries

Group (RLG) Conspectus.[23] Many music collections are organized according to classification schemes other than *LCC* (Dickinson, *ANSCR: The Alpha-Numeric System for Classification of Recordings*, Dewey, etc.),[24] and selectors can use these classifications to describe their collections. Mona L. Scott's *Conversion Tables: LC-Dewey, Dewey-LC*[25] allows Dewey libraries to compare collections with *LCC* libraries. The RLG Music Conspectus subject categories can be used apart from the *LCC* numbers. In fact, the RLG Conspectus provides subject categories for music sound recordings without reference to *LCC* (since the Library of Congress does not classify sound recordings). Different subject categories relevant to a particular collection can also be devised. For example, the following list of subject categories and formats relevant to a master's degree program in jazz performance was compiled without reference to a classification scheme, and was assigned codes to describe the strengths of the existing collection and desired future strengths:

Codes:
   A. Exhaustive, comprehensive;  B. Intensive, extensive;
   C. Beginning research, advanced coursework support;
   D. Undergraduate support level; E. Core level.

| | Existing | Desired |
|---|---|---|
| 1. Scores + parts (jazz) —historic/repertory transcriptions | E | C |
| 2. Scores + parts (jazz) —charts & fakebooks | E | C |
| 3. Scores + parts—American experimentalist traditions | E | C |
| 4. Scores—American vernacular musics | E | C |
| 5. Scores—20th century American | E | D |
| 6. Scores—20th century general | E | D |
| 7. Scores—Western tradition (CE1600–1900) | E | D |
| 8. Books—jazz history | D | C |
| 9. Books—jazz pedagogy, instrument methods | E | C |
| 10. Books—theory & analysis | E | D |
| 11. Books—organology | E | D |
| 12. Books—American vernacular musics | D | D |

|  | Existing | Desired |
|---|:---:|:---:|
| 13. Books—20th century music | D | D |
| 14. Books—world musics | D | D |
| 15. Books—Western tradition (CE1600–1900) | D | D |
| 16. Periodicals—jazz & jazz pedagogy | D | C |
| 17. Periodicals—American vernacular musics | E | C |
| 18. Periodicals—world musics | E | D |
| 19. Sound recordings—historic jazz to 1960 | E | C |
| 20. Sound recordings—contemporary jazz 1960 to present | E | C |
| 21. Sound recordings—American experimental traditions | E | C |
| 22. Sound recordings—American vernacular musics | E | D |
| 23. Sound recordings—20th century music | E | D |
| 24. Sound recordings—world musics | E | D |
| 25. Sound recordings—Western tradition (CE1600–1900) | E | D |

The conspectus approach provides for the inclusion of scope notes and comments to describe "special features of the collection (e.g., chronological and geographical parameters, specific subject emphasis unique to the institution, and inclusion-exclusion boundaries)" and language codes are used to describe inclusions and exclusions based on language.[26] Examples of policies using the conspectus approach to describe existing collection strengths (an assessment function) and current collecting intensities (a development function) can be seen on pages 42–49 of this guide.

### *Narrative statement approach*

The conspectus approach to describing collections and collecting levels in music is criticized because it concentrates on genre and subject content to the exclusion of many other decisions that go into developing music collections, such as which composers and authors are collected; which chronological periods, geographic areas, and stylistic schools are emphasized or excluded; and what types of editions are collected or excluded.[27] In addition, detailed coverage of music outside of the western art tradition is not found in most classification schemes. Some writers of collection development policies for music may find narrative statements more useful than the conspectus method for this section. According to the *Guide for Written Collection Policy Statements*, narrative statements should include, in addition to the factors mentioned in section II:[28]

- Geographical areas covered or excluded, in terms of both intellectual content and publication sources.

- Chronological periods and movements or schools covered or excluded.

- Publication dates collected or excluded.

- Detailed subject descriptions in terms of the library's classification scheme, supplemented with more narrowly defined subsets for aspects of the collection not addressed with enough specificity by the classification scheme. Writers are encouraged to assign the same collecting level codes to each subset as are used in the conspectus approach.[29]

If using the narrative statement approach to section III, it is possible to combine sections II and III of the collection development policy. Chapter 3 contains an example of a policy that uses the narrative statement approach and combines sections II and III. Additional examples of policies using the narrative statement approach to section III are given on pages 49–68 of this guide. The following outline proposes specific issues to consider for possible inclusion in a detailed analysis of collecting levels in music, whether using the conspectus or the narrative statement approach:

A. Books and other textual materials

Considerations for this section include any policies regarding the collection of dissertations and theses, publishers' and dealers' catalogs, textbooks, pamphlets, periodicals (including newspapers), and librettos (including language and translation preferences). Policies regarding the collection of programs and ephemera can also be included here. For example, programs, flyers, and posters for local and regional performances or for specific performers or composers are collected by some libraries and may provide the only documentation of those performances. Include any policies regarding the collection of reference books. Often branch music libraries include some general reference books in their reference collection and note this inclusion in their collection development policy. Any binding preference (hardbound or paperbound) for purchased books can also be stated.

Exclusions or inclusions of books and periodicals according to subject coverage can be noted here. Reading the list of subject categories of writings about music in the RLG Music Conspectus Lines is one approach to thinking about subject inclusions and exclusions.[30]

B. Printed and recorded music
    1. Western art music
        a.  Composers collected systematically, indicate levels (comprehensive, selective)

        For example, local and regional composers may be collected systematically; certain living composers may be collected systematically.

        b.  Emphases or exclusions according to performing medium

        For example, is music for the lute collected? Is choral music collected?

        c.  Emphases or exclusions according to intended use of the music

        For example, is sheet music collected? Are recordings of children's songs collected? Is music intended for performance by children collected? Are hymnals collected?

        d.  Emphases or exclusions according to genre or form

        For example, is ballet music collected? Are opera librettos collected?

e.    Geographic and cultural emphases or exclusions (note that composers working in the western art tradition come from all parts of the world)

f. Historical or chronological emphases or exclusions

g. Performers collected systematically *(recorded music)*
     For example, local performers may be collected systematically.

h. Editions collected or excluded *(printed music)*
     The purposes served by the music collection govern policies to include or exclude types of music editions. For example, libraries with a strong performance constituency will collect editions for performance (scores and parts) but might not emphasize the collection of study scores or scholarly editions. The size of performance ensembles supported by music collections varies among institutions; for example, performance parts may be collected for ensembles of up to eleven performers only, or contrastingly only for large ensembles such as orchestras or bands.
     In some libraries emphasis is placed on the collection of scholarly editions, including composers' collected works, monumental editions, and facsimiles of manuscripts and early editions. Editors of scholarly, or critical, editions study all available primary sources; identify their sources and describe the editorial process; and clearly indicate all editorial markings in the text. Sometimes called "urtext" editions, scholarly editions endeavor to present the composer's original text without editorial changes. Critical editorial process can be applied to performing editions as well as to editions intended for study; some collection policies indicate a preference for scholarly performing editions when available. Different editions of one work may be collected to support historical scholarship, to have both performing and study editions available, and

to provide a variety of editorial interpretations to performers.

Some music publishers specialize in reprint editions, which may be excluded in some collection policies if, for instance, the policy is always to acquire original editions. Because reprint editions are usually lower in price, however, they may be included or emphasized in other policies to provide multiple copies of works in collections used by large numbers of performers or in small collections with limited budgets for scores. Some libraries have policies to include or exclude editions of excerpts of a work when an edition of the full work is in the collection, and some have policies about collecting music in anthologies when possible rather than individually published (or vice versa). Orchestral excerpts for individual instruments may be included or excluded, based on the purpose of the collection.

Policies about collecting or excluding reductions, arrangements, and transcriptions may pertain. For example, vocal scores of operas may be preferred over full scores; piano reductions of orchestral works may be excluded or included, as may transpositions of songs from the original key. Arrangements of works may be excluded unless they are by the original composer. Any policies such as these or others that relate to types of editions collected may be noted in the collection development policy.

2. Music from other traditions: ethnic music, world music, jazz, popular music

Except for popular music from approximately the eighteenth through the early twentieth century, these musics are disseminated more through recordings than through printed music. Types of printed music include pop-folios; fake books; song collections; simplified arrangements (e.g., for piano); transcriptions of recorded performances (jazz and rock); jazz charts; and methods (e.g., how to play blues guitar or how to improvise jazz). Selectors may choose to indicate in the collection development policy which of these types of printed music are emphasized or excluded from their collections, or delineate other types not listed here.

The size and scope of the music collection in many libraries will require this section to be further divided so that various types of non-western and popular music can be treated in more detail. Most library classification schemes do not provide detailed coverage of music outside of the western art tradition. Therefore, supplemental categories or other means of describing collecting levels for these musics is required for many collections. Consulting encyclopedias and other reference works devoted to these musics, as well as histories of specific types of non-western and popular music, will assist the writer of the collection development policy to identify additional relevant subject categories related to the following issues:

a. Styles collected or excluded

b. Performers collected or excluded

c. Ethnic groups represented or excluded, and other cultural emphases or exclusions (especially for ethnic music and world music)

d. Historical, chronological, and geographic emphases or exclusions

e. Composers collected or excluded

f. Other systematic collection criteria
    For example, a selector may systematically collect award-winning recordings, such as those that win a Grammy award, or recordings that are ranked on charts that track sales or radio exposure. Many public libraries systematically collect music for various holidays and for graduation and other ceremonies, and topical music such as songs about baseball.

# 2

# Outline of a Sample Policy with Examples

The following outline contains examples from existing collection development policies for music. Include only those sections or points outlined that pertain to the specific collection and institution under consideration. Not all items will be included in every written collection development policy for music. The examples are not intended as suggestions for wording or inclusion in another collection policy, since every collection policy should be tailored to its specific collection. Rather, the examples are meant to reinforce concepts discussed in chapter 1. For that reason, the examples have been excerpted and edited. In particular, recommendations for the selection of works by specific composers, performers, and authors and references to individual vendors have been deleted. Those decisions should be made by selectors according to the special needs of the collections under their care; this guide does not endorse particular vendors or the inclusion in music collections of certain composers, performers, authors, and publications over others not mentioned in the examples.

# I. Introduction

## A. State the purpose of the policy.

Example 1: *St. Olaf College, Halvorson Music Library* (1998)

Purposes and Aims of the Collection Development Policy for Music

1. The policy aims to establish guiding principles and priorities for planning the growth and maintenance of the collection in music. These principles and priorities should be periodically reevaluated.
2. The policy should facilitate balanced selection and acquisition of new materials as well as identification of materials to be preserved for the permanent library collection.
3. The policy should serve as an important tool for communicating the collecting intentions of the library and the nature and scope of the collection to administrators, faculty and students.
4. The policy should serve as a planning mechanism for allocating the budget.
5. The policy should assist in the identification of strengths and weaknesses in the collection and contribute to the development of cooperative acquisitions efforts with other institutions.

Example 2: *University of Iowa, Rita Benton Music Library* (1991)

Introduction

The purpose of this document is to set guidelines for the procurement of materials needed for the Music Library, so that over succeeding years a collection will be built that will meet the study and research needs of the School of Music faculty and students, and of other members of the University Community who need musical items and information for instruction and research. This document is therefore not primarily a description of the present state of the Library's holdings (although it includes an estimate of that state); rather, it is intended to guide the Library in a consistent development according to the statements below.

## B. Generally describe the institution and define the clientele and programs associated with the collection.

Example 1: *University of Hartford, The Hartt School, Allen Library* (1996)

   User Community
      The music collection supports the curriculum of The Hartt School at various levels and in various fields:

1.  At the **undergraduate** level:
      Bachelor of Music in the fields of Performance, Music Education, Jazz Studies, Music Management, Music History, Composition, Theory, and Music Production & Technology
      Bachelor of Arts with a major or minor in Music, and Performing Arts Management
      Bachelor of Fine Arts with a major in Dance, Music Theatre, and Theatre
      Bachelor of Science in Engineering with a major in Acoustics & Music Technology
2.  At the **masters** level:
      Masters in Music in Performance, Composition, Opera, Music History, Theory, Conducting, and Liturgical Music
      Masters in Music Education
3.  At the **doctoral** level:
      Doctor of Musical Arts in Performance, Composition, Conducting, and Music Education
      Doctor of Philosophy in Music Education
4.  **Diplomas**:
      Undergraduate Diploma in Performance, Composition, and Conducting
      Professional Diploma in Performance, Opera, Conducting, and Composition
      Music Education Certification Programs
5.  The collection supports students studying music in Hartt's Community Division, in the College of Arts and Sciences, and in Hillyer College.

      The primary goal of the collection is to provide materials for students enrolled in Hartt programs and to support faculty preparation for these programs; the collection may also assist faculty in professional research. The collection is a source of information for the musical interests of the University of Hartford community and for the musical community of the Greater Hartford area.

## Example 2: *North Carolina School of the Arts, Semans Library* (1996)

Introduction

The mission of the North Carolina School of the Arts governs all acquisitions policies in the library. NCSA's primary mission of training professional artists and its secondary mission of providing these artists with a well-rounded liberal education, is the driving force behind all acquisition decisions.

For the library, this means that the greatest emphasis is placed upon acquiring items which assist an artist in the performance or creation of art. One example is an emphasis on acquiring scores, method books, basic music history and theory for music students, rather than collecting esoteric works on musicology. There is also an emphasis on the acquisition of materials which visually or aurally present artistic works—including audio recordings, moving image materials, reproductions of photographs and visual artworks, and resources which provide visual documentation of historical people, places, and things.

The North Carolina School of the Arts incorporates a high school program, a four-year college program, and graduate programs in its courses of study. Therefore, the collection development program of the Semans Library must take into account the needs of students enrolled in a general high school curriculum as well as students engaged in highly specialized study in graduate schools.

As a liberal arts institution, NCSA requires its students to complete course work in literature, languages, science, history, social science, and other major disciplines as well as fulfilling their major arts area coursework.

This places another major requirement on the Semans Library's acquisitions program—to provide the basic resource materials in all subject areas needed to support the liberal arts curriculum at the School. The collection development program must balance providing a core collection of basic resources with maintaining and enhancing several specialized arts collections.

Example 3: *University of California at Los Angeles Music Library* (1993)

Programmatic Information
   A. Primary research and instructional programs served by the Music Library
      1. Schools, departments
         Music Department (School of the Arts)
         Musicology Department (College of Letters and Sciences)
         Department of Ethnomusicology and Systematic Musicology (School of the Arts)
      2. Descriptive information
         a. Undergraduate concentration
            B.A. degrees in Music, Musicology, Ethnomusicology
         b. Graduate degrees offered
            M.A. degrees in Music, Musicology, Ethnomusicology
            M.F.A. degree in Music
            Ph.D. degrees in Music, Musicology, Ethnomusicology
      3. UCLA specific programmatic information
         a. Profile of school or department
            The Music Library serves 135 graduate and 230 undergraduate music majors and 85 faculty within the three music departments, and about 1,800 non-major music students enrolled in undergraduate music courses each quarter.
            i. Subjects emphasized
               Ethnomusicology: "study of all styles of music in the world, including popular music, jazz, and . . . world musics."
               Systematic musicology: "perspectives of aesthetics and philosophy, music theory, acoustics, sociology, psychology, organology, and semiotics."
               Music: "program of practical, theoretical and historical studies with core

curriculum of theory, history, analysis, and individual and group performance."

Musicology: "history and literature of the art music of Europe and the Americas."

—UCLA General Catalog, 1991–1992

ii. Subjects excluded or low interest

Not applicable

B. Other research and instructional programs served

1. Schools, departments

School of the Arts

Dance Department

World Arts and Cultures Department

School of Theater, Film and Television

Film and Television Department

Theater Department

College of Letters and Sciences

African Area Studies

Afro-American Studies

American Indian Studies

Chicano Studies

Folklore and Mythology

Islamic Studies

Latin American Studies

[Note: All of these interdisciplinary programs include music faculty and courses.]

2. Descriptive information

a. Undergraduate concentration

B.A. degrees in Dance, World Arts and Cultures, Film and Television, Theater, African Area Studies, Afro-American Studies, American Indian Studies, Folklore and Mythology, Islamic Studies, and Latin American Studies

b. Graduate degrees offered

M.A. degrees in Dance, Film and Television, Theater, African Area Studies, American Indian Studies, Latin American Studies, and Islamic Studies

M.F.A. degrees in Dance, Film and Television, Theater

Ph.D. degrees in Theater, Film and Television, Dance (in conjunction with UC

             Riverside), Folklore and Mythology, and Islamic Studies

   c. Other

        American Indian Studies Center

        Asian American Studies Center

        Center for Afro-American Studies

        Center for Medieval and Renaissance Studies

        Center for Seventeenth and Eighteenth Century Studies

        Center for the Study of Comparative Folklore & Mythology

        Chicano Studies Research Center

        Institute of American Cultures

        Latin American Center

        William Andrews Clark Library Seminar and Studies Program

3. UCLA specific programmatic information

   a. Emphasis of school or department

        Emphases include performance and production in each discipline.

   b. Subjects excluded or low interest

        Not applicable

## C. State the mission and goals of the collection management and development program.

Example 1: *University of Western Ontario, Music Library* (1990)

> The general purpose of this Library is to make available material which will support the University's aims, goals, and functions in the field of music.
>    The following are, in order of importance, the principal collection objectives of the Music Library:
> > A. To collect material which will support the curricular needs of the library users.
> > B. To collect material which will, in general, support research and advanced study.
> > C. To collect material which will assist the library users' intellectual and recreational interests which may or may not be directly related to the curricula.

Example 2: see page 71, "Mission and Goals"

## D. Include or refer to the institutional library system's official statements about intellectual freedom, censorship, and copyright issues.

Example 1: *North Carolina School of the Arts, Semans Library* (1996)

> Policies on intellectual freedom/censorship issues as they relate to acquisitions.
> The Library does not condone censorship in any form. All materials are available for use by students, faculty, staff, and local patrons regardless of the patron's age, gender, political, or other affiliations, or any other factor. Limitations on the use of certain materials—such as non-circulating closed reserves or recordings and moving image materials are not to be based on the content of the material. Rather, it is the format, fragility, irreplaceable value, or uniqueness of an item which should dictate its placement in special collections such as closed reserve. Items which have a history of being at high risk for theft or defacement, such as certain popular magazines, may also be kept in closed stacks (such as behind the circulation desk) to provide better security, but the availability of these materials is to be made clear, and these materials are to be made available to any patron upon request.

Example 2: *Columbus Metropolitan Library, Main Library* (1994)

> Controversial Materials
> CML supports the Library Bill of Rights and the American Film and Video Association's Freedom to View statement endorsed by ALA. It is the library's responsibility to provide broad access to a diverse collection of resources that are representative of our thought and culture including those in media formats. The library resists labeling or prejudging materials based on the opinions of one person or special interest group. While those opinions will always be considered in the materials review process, they cannot be the sole basis for whether to include a specific title in the collection.
> The media collection represents the interests of a diverse metropolitan community, just as the print collection does. Therefore, media resources are evaluated by the same general criteria as

print. Materials may be included which contain frank treatments of situations, language, or images that could be objectionable to some. These materials may be included in the collection if they meet general selection criteria. The library has the responsibility to protect the rights of mature or sophisticated viewers and listeners.

The library does recognize the powerful impact of the visual message. In addition to the general materials selection criteria, reasonable guidelines will be used to help identify AV materials that are appropriate for the public library collection. For example, any feature film receiving an R rating or lower is automatically considered part of contemporary popular culture. However, film editions receiving an NC-17 rating will not be selected for the video collection, since they exclude viewing by a general audience. Also, any music played on open airwaves is considered to meet community standards. Materials that fall outside these areas will be considered on an individual basis.

## E. Provide a brief overview of the collection, including prominent features of its history if appropriate, and the location(s) of its holdings (including remote storage).

Example 1: *University of Illinois at Urbana-Champaign, Music Library* (1998)

Overview of library and its collections

1.  On 16 February 1944, a branch music library consisting of a reserve collection of 250 titles opened on the second floor of Smith Memorial Hall. By this date, the University Library had already assembled a collection of some 15,000 volumes of printed music and books about music, and over thirty years music collections and services spread throughout Smith Hall. In August 1974, the Music Library moved into its present quarters in the north wing of the School of Music building, occupying 23,000 square feet of floor space over two floors.

2.  The library's collections are particularly strong in reference materials, historical musicology and ethnomusicology monographs, music education dissertations on microfilm, and recordings of nineteenth- and early-twentieth-century music. The library collects selectively in the areas of music therapy, music business, and recent popular music.

    3.  Collection locations:
- a. The majority of the library's holdings are located in the Music Library, north wing of Music Building, 1114 West Nevada St.
- b. Ensembles collections: Smith Memorial Hall, Room 306.
- c. Remote storage: University Press Building, 1325 S. Oak Street.
- d. Approximately 14,000 music-related volumes are housed in the Main Library and the Undergraduate Library, and approximately 1,300 titles are housed in the Rare Books and Special Collections Library to ensure their security.

Example 2: see page 71, "Overview of the Collection"

## F. Identify persons responsible for building and maintaining the collection.

Example 1: *St. Olaf College, Halvorson Music Library* (1998)

Final responsibility for materials selection rests with the music librarian and the library director. However, faculty should play a major role in selecting material. The music librarian will coordinate and supplement faculty efforts.

Example 2: *North Carolina School of the Arts, Semans Library* (1996)

Acquisitions criteria
The criteria for selection of materials is based on the following: 1) Faculty requests or recommendations. 2) Student, staff, or other patron requests or recommendations. Note: All requests are evaluated by the library staff involved in collection development. In some cases, especially in keeping with the equitable distribution of funds across the disciplines, a specific request will not be placed into the acquisitions file. (For example, the librarian may find that the library already has a sufficient amount of material on a specific topic or already has other editions or versions of a particular work.) The requester will be notified as to why the item will not be acquired. 3) Research and reference needs, as outlined in faculty (or other) descriptions of current or future courses and projects. 4) Re-

search and reference needs, as demonstrated by patron queries and reference questions. 5) Other needs in the collection, especially major gaps in the coverage of certain disciplines, topics, formats, etc., as determined by the librarians in their surveys of the collection, and by recommendations from patrons. 6) Standard acquisition tools, such as subject-area bibliographies and research guides. 7) Professional literature and other review and information sources. 8) Special consideration is given to items which receive major awards.

## G. Outline the relationship of the collection development policy to collection management programs for preservation, storage, replacement, deselection, and access (including the procurement of equipment and technical support for the provision of access).

Example 1: *University of California at Los Angeles Music Library* (1993)

Preservation Policy
The Music Library consults and cooperates with the UCLA Library Preservation Officer's program. Books and scores are generally bound and scores are housed on special shelving slotted for supports to keep them upright. Recordings are shelved upright, and have use restrictions for their preservation. Record cleaning equipment accompanies LP recordings charged out for listening. Archival materials are housed in acid-free, buffered folders, and are stored in sturdy, acid-free document boxes.

Example 2: *North Carolina School of the Arts, Semans Library* (1996)

Policy on the Disposal of Library Materials from the Semans Library.
Over time, many library materials can become outdated, containing erroneous or misleading information which does not have an intrinsic historic value. Library materials are also subject to irreparable damage and deterioration. For this reason it is necessary to maintain a "weeding" program in library collections. The purpose of such a program is to evaluate and to remove from the library collection any item which is judged to be no longer of infor-

mational use, is being replaced by an updated edition, or is damaged beyond repair.

## Example 3: *St. Olaf College, Halvorson Music Library* (1998)

Deselection and Preservation of the Collection

1. Deselection (Weeding)

   The relevance of materials in the library may change over time. Periodic weeding of the collection is necessary to identify items which no longer fit the criteria for inclusion in the collection. Extra copies of titles for which there is no longer demand should also be weeded.

2. Preservation

   Titles which are not weeded are in fact chosen for permanent status in the collection. The logical step is to ensure that these materials are in lasting physical condition. Routine binding, rebinding, replacement, or microfilming of titles in poor condition should be systematically undertaken. Such maintenance is an essential part of collection development insuring against the need to purchase expensive reprints at a later date and against complete loss of significant titles for which no replacement in any form is available.

## H. Describe cooperative collecting agreements and consortial agreements (including interlibrary loan).

## Example 1: *New York University, Bobst Library* (1995)

A cooperative agreement between NYU and Columbia University for music acquisitions (begun in 1993) has already had an important effect on local collecting patterns and has been incorporated into the current-collecting-intensity levels in Part VI below. Under the agreement, NYU assumes the primary, continuing responsibility for 1) Verdi (all print and recorded materials), 2) experimental music, especially "downtown" music (recordings), 3) musical theatre (scores and recordings), and 4) Latin American music (recordings); Columbia takes responsibility for the intensive, systematic acquisition of contemporary-music scores. The two institutions will also collaborate on expensive, one-time purchases, such as facsimiles and large sets.

In a more general way, the music policy takes into account the proximity of the Performing Arts Research Library of New York Public Library and NYU's membership in the Research Libraries Group, such that patrons with specialized research needs for materials not collected by Bobst are still adequately served through interlibrary loan or referral.

## Example 2: *Duke University, Music Library* (1995)

As a member of the university community of the North Carolina Triangle region, Duke has formed special cooperative agreements with North Carolina State at Raleigh and the University of North Carolina at Chapel Hill. An informal collection development agreement between the music libraries at UNC/CH and Duke concerning the duplication of expensive serials, sets, and primary source materials (for example, films and facsimiles of manuscripts) is ongoing.

## I. Delineate procedures and a timeline for regular review and revision of the collection development policy.

Example: *University of Iowa, Rita Benton Music Library* (1991)

Revisions, Amendments, and Expiration
This document will be subject to review at all times. In any case, it will expire each three-year period if it is not re-endorsed by the University Libraries Administration and the School of Music.

This document may also be amended or revised whenever there is a consensus among the aforesaid that it should be so altered to better fulfill the purposes for which the Music Library exists.

## II. Summary of the scope of coverage at current collecting levels

Example 1: *Columbus Metropolitan Library, Main Library* (1994)

RECORDED MUSIC COLLECTION
. . . Music is a documentation of history, especially since the advent of recordings. When vinyl records were the predominant format in use, they were purchased by the library. The current formats selected are audio

cassettes and compact discs. As these formats continue to evolve, library purchasing will adjust accordingly.

This collection represents a unique resource in the Central Ohio area. Many resources included here are not found anywhere else in the county. The Main Library collection is readily available to customers throughout the county through the regular library online reserve system.

Present goals of the division in selecting music are to provide a resource for entertainment, education, cultural needs, and research on a limited level. Selection of contemporary recordings will concentrate on maintaining currency of materials through approval plans. The selection of multicultural recordings will also continue to be expanded. In addition, many purchases will be coordinated with the Humanities, Fine Arts and Recreation Division to match our recordings with their sheet music collection. Recordings by local artists will be given special attention.

The scope of this collection includes a representation of many commercially available types of music. The depth of each category—as well as the format of recordings chosen—are based on anticipated popularity, extent of repertoire, level of technical excellence in recording and packaging, and general use as identified by stock turnover reports. Particular emphasis will be placed on acquiring a basic repertoire of all types of music. Many purchases are demand driven according to customer requests and quantity of outstanding reserves.

Because of losses due to theft and damage, certain areas of the recorded music collection will require constant maintenance. However, in those high loss areas (currently rock, rap, gospel, and reggae), replacements will be selective and limited to significant recordings by recognized artists.

The play lists being used by local radio stations are also considered as selection criteria. The library does not attempt to be the first resource for contemporary popular music, however, since it is so easily available on the retail market.

Since children's music is selected and shelved in the Center for Discovery, all AV music selections are based on adult standards. As with video, parents are expected to assume responsibility for guiding their child's choices.

Music involves a number of shelving considerations that are unique due to format and packaging. Recordings may be shelved separately from accompanying print material which may be in HFAR. Multi-part titles may also be packaged separately and circulated individually.

SELECTION TOOLS
Catalogs
    Trade service catalogs
    Manufacturers catalogs

New release information from distributors
Reviews in journals
Buying guides (discographies; guides to various genres of recorded music)
Vendor-initiated approval plan based on specific charts
Patron requests

## Example 2: *University of Hartford, The Hartt School, Allen Library* (1996)

General Guidelines
*Geographical.* There is no limitation on geographical areas collected. Emphasis is on the Western art tradition and jazz, although materials of Latin America, Asia and Africa are also collected. Vernacular music is collected, with geographic emphasis on the United States.

*Linguistic.* Music and sound recordings are collected for their intrinsic musical value, regardless of the language of their texts and notes. Writings about music are collected principally in English; significant materials in Western European languages are acquired when equivalent materials are not available in English. These include reference, historical, critical and analytical works; composers' correspondence, and theoretical writings.

*Chronological.* There is no limitation on chronological periods collected. Materials from all periods to the present are included. In some instances retrospective purchasing is advisable for historical and comparative purposes. Reprints are often purchased for reasons of durability.

Types of Materials Collected
Music; sound recordings of music; videocassettes of musical productions and master classes; laser discs; interactive media; CD-ROMs; monographs; periodicals; serials; proceedings of associations, conferences, congresses, and societies; newsletters; Festschriften; reference works; publisher and trade catalogs; electronic resources.

*Music*: printed editions of scores, piano reductions, and arrangements, performance materials for works requiring one performer per part, and collected and historical editions are acquired; facsimile editions of composer manuscripts are acquired whenever possible.

*Sound recordings*: LP discs form the bulk of the collection, although few are being added to the collection. CDs are increasing in number rapidly. Cassettes are acquired of Hartt concerts, for some reserve needs, and for theater studies. Reel-to-reel tapes and 78 RPMs are not being added to the collection.

*Videocassettes*: VHS is the library standard.

*Laser discs*: It is anticipated that laser discs will be collected in the near future.

*Writings on music*: Printed formats are preferred; microforms are acquired for important materials not available in printed format, for periodical titles that are not bindable, and for dissertations.

*Doctoral dissertations*: In printed or microformat, these may be acquired to support graduate programs.

*Electronic formats*: CD-ROMs of reference materials are acquired whenever possible and appropriate. Mixed media CD-ROMs are generally acquired as published. Online access is provided whenever possible. Access to electronic formats is expected to increase for appropriate materials (such as reference information).

Exclusions

Programmed texts and other workbook type materials; juvenalia; "how to" books; popular biographies; non-music sound recordings and videocassettes (except where needed for the dance and theatre programs); sets of performance materials for large ensembles are not acquired.

Deaccessioning

Deaccessioning is governed by the criteria set forth in the LLR Collection Development Policy. It is undertaken for the purpose of refining and upgrading the collection. Deaccessioned materials are disposed of by sale in a library book sale, sale to or exchange with another library, or donation to a suitable institution.

Materials may be removed from the collection for the following reasons:

1. The physical condition warrants it.
2. Part of the item is missing and cannot be replaced.
3. The contents are outdated and superceded by another edition or title.

Other Resources Available on Campus

Sets of band, choral, and orchestral parts are maintained by the Orchestra and Choral Libraries. Materials documenting the history of music at The Hartt School are housed in the University Archives. Tapes of all events of the Hartt School of Music are housed in the Hartt Recording Studio. Materials related to music education are maintained in the Music Education Resource Library. Dance periodicals and videos are located at the Library of the School for the Hartford Ballet. Materials on dance, theater, and technology are also located in the Mortensen Library.

Notes
1. Every effort is made to coordinate the collecting of music and sound recordings. In addition, duplication in each of these collections is pursued deliberately in order to acquire the best editions and performances currently available, as well as a variety of performances.
2. Many of the music materials are regularly used in classrooms and rehearsals. This constant and welcome wear means that replacement of worn materials is an important ongoing need for the music collection.
3. Multiple copies of the most important and most heavily used works are acquired. If several good editions/performances of such works are available, more than one (but not all available editions and performances) is acquired.

Gifts

　　　Gifts are accepted and retained at the discretion of the music librarian. Gifts will be accepted without restriction on their use or disposition. In general, materials will be added to the collection if they fall within current collection policy guidelines and if the physical condition of the individual items is deemed suitable for library use. Gifts may be maintained as a collection. Books and scores added to the collection are marked with a bookplate acknowledging the donor. Items not added to the collection are disposed of as appropriate. This may include placement in a book sale, sale to or exchange with another library, or donation to a suitable institution.

　　　Gifts are acknowledged by the music librarian. Appraisals or estimates of value cannot be provided. Gifts are not accepted on a conditional basis and will not be returned to the donor.

Collection Profile (11/96)
　　　No. of course subjects:  730 (458 undergraduate; 272 graduate)
　　　No. of undergraduate majors:  450
　　　No. of graduate majors:  100 FT; 125 PT
　　　No. of Community Division registrations:  1,800
　　　No. of faculty:  130 Collegiate Division; 100 Community Division
　　　Size of collection:  75,815 vols.
　　　No. of serial subscriptions:  346
　　　Uncataloged or special materials:  approx. 1,500 uncat. items; publishers and trade catalogs file
　　　Circulation:  39,000 per year (6,530 in-house pick-ups)
　　　No. of cataloged titles added per year:  1,851

## Example 3: *Duke University, Music Library* (1995)

DESCRIPTION OF THE COLLECTION

. . . The collection is quite strong in the area of Western European art music and contains almost all of the standard scholarly editions, including complete and collected composer editions, national monuments, and genre sets dealing with the music of the Western world. The standard reference works, histories, and biographies of Western music are also well represented. The collection is less strong in the area of scholarly journals (although subscriptions for almost all of the standard titles in English are maintained) and in the area of practical performance scores, where some lacunae exist with regard to the "standard" performance repertory.

For research purposes, current and retrospective collection development priorities have been placed on the following subject areas:

1. Books and scores dealing with keyboard music (i.e., music for organ, harpsichord, or clavichord, for the most part) before 1750
2. Opera scores and literature on opera
3. Iconography and organology (i.e., music in art and also the science and construction of musical instruments)
4. The printing and publishing of music, with emphasis on Viennese music from the time of Haydn to Mahler (i.e., ca. 1750–1910)
5. British music (including, to some extent, the music of colonial British America)
6. The literature on performance practice
7. The literature on computers in music and computer software related to music

The rationale for these priorities has been derived from an assessment of the existing strengths of the collection, the music curriculum, the inter-disciplinary mission of the university, and current research interests of faculty and students.

COLLECTING GUIDELINES

*Chronological.* There are no strict chronological restrictions. Musical artifacts and iconography preserved from ancient civilizations down to the graphic notations and electronic synthesis of sound of the present day are appropriate subjects for collection. However, since the volume of publication on musical subjects dating roughly from the European invention of printing to the present day is decidedly heavier than for the previous periods, the *de facto* chronological emphasis is on the most recent several hundred years.

*Geographical.* Generally speaking, because of the past development of the collection and also the present emphases of the music curriculum, the highest priority for collection development is likely to remain on the art music and music literature of Western Europe, especially Great Britain, France, Germany, Austria, Italy, the Scandinavian countries, and the Iberian Peninsula. North America, Central America, South America, and Eastern Europe (including Russia), along with Southern and Southeastern Asia, form a second echelon. Eastern Asia, Africa, and other areas of the world form a third. Despite these general rankings, it is the intent that representative and important materials from all regions and countries will be acquired.

Among the cities of the world, Vienna has probably the highest priority because of its bibliographical prominence within the Weinmann Collection. Other cities with high priorities include Paris, London, Berlin, Leipzig, and Rome.

*Languages.* The clear emphasis will be on modern Roman-alphabet languages emanating from Western Europe, with English first and foremost, followed by German, French, Italian, Spanish, and Dutch in roughly that order. Primary source texts in Latin will also have a high priority. Some Scandinavian languages and Eastern European languages will be covered selectively.

Materials in non-Roman alphabets will be considered and acquired very selectively, with some emphasis placed on Greek, Hebrew, and Cyrillic texts, followed by those in Chinese, Japanese, and Korean. The availability of English summaries or translations of these materials will normally enhance the collection development priority of an individual item in this category.

*Format.* The matter of physical format is one of some complexity in music. There is the usual array of printed text publications (monographs, serials, pamphlets, etc.), to which must be added materials predominantly in musical notation (including the conductor's or full score, the piano-vocal score, individual instrumental or vocal parts, the study or miniature score, etc.). There are also sound recordings of various kinds—from the acoustic cylinder developed by Thomas Edison in the 1870s to the very recently marketed DAT (digital audio tape—and visual media, some linked with computers (videotapes, laser discs, CD-ROM materials, and the like). For the purposes of collection development, all of the printed formats are important; in the media/computer sector, the acquisition of the newest formats will depend on the availability of hardware or playback equipment.

The question of individual parts for instrumental ensemble music (and to a lesser extent vocal ensemble music) looms large in the collection development activities of many music libraries. It is customary to "draw the line" at about nine to twelve parts, i.e., to collect (if available) individual parts for titles that require up to that many and no more, under the assumption that (1) almost all works in the standard chamber music repertory are thereby subsumed, (2) works with many parts are physically difficult to manage and account for, and (3) there will be a separate library for the needs of ensembles that normally perform works with many parts (e.g., large choirs and orchestras). The guidelines for Duke are to acquire up to twelve parts and, almost equally important, to acquire parts along with the score whenever available.

When both the full or conductor's score and the piano-vocal score are available for a given title, preference will normally be given to the full score, but in many cases, it will be desirable to have both.

In the non-print categories, preference will often be given to materials in the latest proven technologies, when playback equipment is available. CDs are currently the preferred format for sound recordings, but the acquisition of LPs is not entirely excluded, particularly if no other format is available. Audio cassettes and video cassettes are acquired very selectively. DATs, CD-ROMs, and laser discs are under consideration.

Other recording formats, such as 78 rpm, 45 rpm, reel-to-reel tape, and even cylinder recordings can be received very selectively as gifts but will rarely be purchased. Piano rolls and other similar recording devices designed to be used with mechanical reproducing instruments are not normally collected.

*Editions and recorded versions.* Printed titles in what has come to be called the standard repertory are often available in two or more editions, sometimes in the so-called "urtext" version (which usually distinguishes unedited from edited portions of the musical text) in addition to one or more other versions with various editorial emendations and comments. (Performers sometimes prefer "urtext" versions over others.) It is frequently desirable to have more than one edition of the same work.

Solo vocal works are sometimes issued in different keys, and for selected editions of standard repertory items, it is desirable to have works in all the available keys.

In a similar vein, it is frequently desirable to have more than one recorded version of a standard work. For the listener or viewer, it can be instructive to hear or see various interpretations.

*Stylistic considerations.* Because of the general nature of the academic program (which covers the current curriculum, current research and compositional interests, and the repertoire of applied music study and performances sponsored by the music department), much emphasis goes to Western art or concert music, sometimes referred to as "classical" music, from the era of Western liturgical chant up to the present. Also to be considered for the collection are representative examples in any format of folk or traditional musics and popular musics from around the world.

*Music disciplines and collecting levels.* The scholarly study of music has been in the past subdivided into various branches, typically including, for example, musicology, music theory, ethnomusicology, and music education. Of these, the one clearly not represented in the curriculum is music education, which for that reason will be collected only very selectively, i.e., at a basic level. In this context, musicology, music theory, and ethnomusicology in general will be collected at the curricular support level. The areas of emphasis mentioned previously (see Description of the Collection) will be collected at the research level. No subjects are currently being collected at the comprehensive (i.e., most intensive and exhaustive) level, with the exception of primary source materials in the area of keyboard music before 1700.

## COLLECTING METHODS

*Tools.* A wide variety of selection tools, including bibliographical listings in journals, publishers' brochures, dealers' catalogs, card or slip services, antiquarian and out-of-print dealers' catalogs, and standard bibliographies are to be consulted.

*Methodology.* Collection development should involve the community of users of the library. The library accepts suggestions and requests from that community and especially from those faculty members teaching courses within the Department of Music. Members of the library staff with collection development or bibliographical responsibilities systematically read and evaluate the large number of incoming materials pertaining to new, out-of-print, and antiquarian publications in order to make decisions about acquisitions, keeping in mind (1) the priorities and guidelines established for collection development and (2) the status of the pertinent budget lines throughout the fiscal year. Library staff also assist in the preparation of standing order or approval plan profiles and survey materials received according to these plans.

## III. Detailed analysis of the collection

Example 1: *University of Hartford, The Hartt School, Allen Library* (1996) Note: this example of the conspectus approach describes existing and desired collection levels.

Collection Level Definitions
    A. *Comprehensive Level.* Doctoral level and possibly beyond. All currently published relevant material. Extensive retrospective purchasing as appropriate to the field.
    B. *Beginning Research Level.* Up to and including the master's level. Significant current primary sources; some retrospective purchasing; in languages in which significant research is being carried on other than primary language.
    C. *Teaching or Undergraduate Level.* Standard works; selected current works (mostly in English unless nature of the subject gives primacy to another language); basic reference works and journals; retrospective purchasing mainly limited to standard works.
    D. *Reference Level.* Supports occasional general needs for information about subjects not offered as part of the curriculum.

| Detailed Subject Areas | Collection Levels | |
|---|---|---|
| | Existing | Desirable |
| MUSIC | | |
| Church Music | D | D |
| Dance | D | C |
| Ethnomusicology | | |
| —American folk | D+ | D+ |
| —Other | D- | D- |
| Facsimile editions | C-D | B |
| Historical anthologies, monumental series, collected works of individual composers | B | A-B |

| Detailed Subject Areas | Collection Levels | |
|---|---|---|
| | Existing | Desirable |
| Instrumental and vocal music | | |
| —performing editions for solos-small chamber ensemble | B-C | A-B |
| —scores and study/rehearsal arrangements for band, chorus, orchestra, and chamber music | B-C | A-B |
| Jazz | – | C-D |
| Music education classroom materials | in Music Ed Resource Lib. | |
| Music theater | B-C | B |
| Opera | B+ | B+ |
| Pedagogy | C | B-C |
| Popular Music | | |
| —United States | D | D |
| —Other | – | – |
| | | |
| VIDEO CASSETTES | | |
| Concerts & recitals | D | C |
| Dance | in Library of the SHB | |
| Ethnomusicology materials | D | C-D |
| Films (artfilms, documentary, etc.) | in Mortensen Library | |
| Jazz | D | C |
| Master classes | D | C |
| Music theater | D | ? |
| Opera | C | B |
| Pedagogy | D | D |
| Popular music | D | D |
| | | |
| SOUND RECORDINGS | | |
| Church Music | D | D |
| Ethnomusicology | | |
| —American folk | D | C+ |
| —Other | D | C-D |
| Film music | D | D |
| Instrumental and vocal music | B-C | A-B |
| Jazz | C | B |
| Music education materials | D | D |
| | Also in Music Ed. Res. Lib. | |

| Detailed Subject Areas | Collection Levels | |
|---|---|---|
| | Existing | Desirable |
| Music theater | C | B |
| Opera | B | B+ |
| Popular music | | |
| —United States | D | C-D |
| —Other | D | D |
| | | |
| WRITINGS ON MUSIC | | |
| Acoustics & technology | D | C |
| | | Also in Science Coll. |
| Aesthetics and philosophy | C-D | B-C |
| Church | C-D | C-D |
| Ethnomusicology | | |
| —American folk | D | C |
| —Other | D | C-D |
| Film | D | D |
| History and criticism of music | B-C | A-B |
| Jazz | C- | B-C |
| Music appreciation | C | C |
| Music education | C | A-B |
| Music management | C- | B-C |
| Music theater | C- | B-C |
| Performance practice | B-C | A-B |
| Popular music | C-D | C+ |
| Reference books | B | A-B |
| Related performing arts | D | C |
| Theory and composition | B | A |

Example 2: *University of Iowa, Rita Benton Music Library* (1991)
Note: this example of the conspectus approach describes existing collection strength, current collecting intensity, and desired collecting intensity, and uses Research Libraries Group Conspectus terms and categories.

Collection categories:

0   *Out of scope*: not purchased, and not kept if given (except as noted).
1   *Minimal level*: only basic works are purchased; gifts will be kept.

2   *Basic information level*: a collection of up-to-date general materials that serve to introduce and define a subject and to indicate the varieties of information available elsewhere. Not sufficient to support any courses or independent study in the subject.

3   *Instructional support level:* adequate to support undergraduate and lower level graduate instruction, or sustained independent study.

4   *Research level:* includes the major published source materials required for dissertations and independent research.

5   *Comprehensive level:* the aim is exhaustiveness.

ECS = Existing collection strength; CCI = Current collecting intensity; DCI = Desired collecting intensity

Language codes, where applicable: E = English; W = other common western European languages. (Note: language codes are not used as per RLG.)

*See the appropriate note following the table.

|  | ECS | CCI | DCI |
|---|---|---|---|
| Reference books (dictionaries, encycl., library catalogs, etc.) | 4E,4W | 4E,3W | 4E,4W |
| Histories, biographies, studies, periodicals in the following areas: |  |  |  |
| Ancient music | 3E,2W | 4E,1W | 4E,3W |
| Medieval and Renaissance | 3E,3W | 4E,1W | 4E,3W |
| Baroque | 3E,2W | 4E,1W | 4E,3W |
| Classical | 3E,3W | 4E,1W | 4E,3W |
| Romantic | 4E,4W | 4E,1W | 4E,3W |
| Contemporary "art" music | 4E,3W | 4E,1W | 4E,3W |
| American music | 4E,2W | 4E,1W | 4E,1W |
| Iowa music | 3E | 3E | 4E |
| Jazz | 3E,1W | 4E,1W | 4E,2W |

| | ECS | CCI | DCI |
|---|---|---|---|
| Popular music | 2E,0W | 3E,0W | 3E,1W |
| Music theory and composition | 3E,3W | 4E,1W | 4E,3W |
| Church and choral music | 3E,2W | 4E,1W | 4E,3W |
| | ECS | CCI | DCI |
| Music education (excluding curriculum materials) | 3E,1W | 3E,0W | 3E,1W |
| Music therapy | 2E,2W | 4E,1W | 4E,1W |
| Ethnomusicology | 1E,1W | 2E,1W | 3E,2W |
| "Appreciation" and introductory texts (MT6) [accept as gifts, only to level 2] | 2E,1W | 1E,0W | 2E,1W |
| Aesthetics and psychology of music | 3E,3W | 4E,1W | 4E,4W |
| Collections of essays, Festschriften, congress reports, etc. | 3E,3W | 3E,1W | 4E,3W |
| Theses and dissertations | 2E,1W | 2E,1W | 2E,1W |
| Trade catalogs and lists (will accept gifts) | 0 | 0 | 0 |
| Program books of major orchestras, other "program notes" books ("hermeneutics") | 4E,3W | 3E,1W | 4E,2W |
| *Libretti | 3 | 2 | 4 |
| Illustrations [apart from iconographical publications] | 0 | 0 | 0 |
| *Music scores: collected editions | 4 | 4 | 4 |
| study, traditional repertoire | 3 | 3 | 4 |
| *contemporary music | 2 | 3 | 4 |
| *conducting scores | 2 | 2 | 2 |

| | ECS | CCI | DCI |
|---|---|---|---|
| Performance music: | | | |
| solo instrumental | | | |
| (including solo + | | | |
| keyboard): | | | |
| **SEE separate list** | | | |
| **below** | | | |
| *chamber (parts), to | | | |
| 9/10 instr. | 2 | 3 | 4 |
| songs with kb | | | |
| with/without | | | |
| additional instr. | 3 | 2 | 4 |
| vocal duets, trios, etc. | | | |
| (as above) | 1 | 2 | 3 |
| *single songs ("sheet | | | |
| music") | 1 | 1 | 2 |
| choral works, major | 3 | 3 | 4 |
| *choral works, octavo- | | | |
| type [accept gifts] | 2 | 1 | 2 |
| Song collections, popular | 1 | 2 | 2 |
| Folk-song collections: | | | |
| English- and standard | 2 | 1 | 3 |
| European-languages | | | |
| other | 2 | 0 | 2 |
| Manuscripts (sketches, | | | |
| scores, letters) | | | |
| [*encourage* as gifts] | 1 | 0 | 2 |
| Facsimiles, manuscript | 4 | 2 | 4 |
| Facsimiles, early printed | | | |
| works | 3 | 2 | 4 |
| Microfilms of musical | | | |
| sources | 3 | 1 | 3 |
| Hymnals | 2 | 1 | 3 |
| Service music, Christian | 2 | 1 | 3 |
| Synagogue music | 1 | 1 | 2 |
| Instrumental methods | 3 | 1 | 2 |
| Instrumental studies, | | | |
| etudes | 3 | 1 | 3 |
| General books on | | | |
| instrumental | 2E,2W | 2E,0W | 3E,2W |
| instruction | | | |
| Books on singing | 3E,4W | 3E,1W | 3E,3W |

Notes on various categories:

**Libretti:** no attempt is made to define various language combinations; collection levels should reflect availability in English translation.

**Music scores:** refers to formats not usable for performance (except as conducting scores). Most "scores" are in the succeeding categories.

**Contemporary music:** items acquired largely through approval plans.

**Conducting scores:** plus many in the collected editions and contemporary categories.

**Performance music, chamber:** the wind chamber music collection, maintained by the faculty, contains a large amount of music that is appropriate for eventual inclusion in the Music Library collection; an effort will be made to avoid duplication of these items.

**Single songs** and **octavo choral:** many important composers publish in these formats; preference for the songs will be to wait for future collected volumes, whereas octavos tend not to be similarly republished, so should eventually be purchased. Gifts should be actively sought.

PERFORMANCE MUSIC, SOLO INSTRUMENTAL
(The entire family of any single instrument is implied.)

|                   | ECS | CCI | DCI |
| ----------------- | --- | --- | --- |
| organ             | 4   | 4   | 4   |
| piano/harpsichord | 3   | 4   | 4   |
| violin            | 3   | 3   | 4   |
| viola             | 2   | 2   | 4   |
| violoncello       | 2   | 2   | 4   |
| double bass       | 1   | 2   | 4   |
| flute             | 3   | 4   | 4   |
| recorder          | 1   | 1   | 2   |
| oboe/English horn | 1   | 2+  | 4   |
| clarinet          | 2   | 2   | 4   |
| bassoon           | 1   | 2   | 4   |

|                     | ECS | CCI | DCI |
|---------------------|-----|-----|-----|
| saxophone           | 1   | 2   | 4   |
| horn                | 1   | 2+  | 4   |
| trumpet/cornet      | 1   | 2+  | 4   |
| trombone            | 1   | 2   | 4   |
| tuba                | 1   | 2   | 4   |
| harp                | 1   | 1   | 1   |
| guitar/lute         | 2   | 3   | 2   |
| other plucked instr.| 1   | 1   | 2   |
| percussion, pitched | 1   | 2   | 3   |
| percussion, unpitched | 1 | 2   | 3   |

Note: In the ECS (existing collection strength) column, the numbers 1 and 2 do not, in this case, signify "basic works" and "up-to-date general materials" respectively; they are based solely on the number of items, most of which tend more to be "fringe" rather than basic repertoire.

Example 3: *Bowling Green State University Sound Recordings Archives* (1995) Note: this example of the narrative statement approach describes the existing collection and current collecting intensity.

This policy is arranged by genres and prioritized by the collection's commitment to the university and faculty needs. Priorities also relate to collections that exist in other institutions and their accessibility to scholars and their needs.

*First priorities* represent comprehensive collection building activity related directly to those genres treated in University courses. In most instances BGSU is already the most comprehensive or the *only* existing academic collection of certain genres, such as rock, disco, comedy, and kiddie.

*Second priorities* represent those genres that relate to courses and research at BGSU but only on a lower request level. In some instances other institutional collections already exist with similar holdings. For this priority BGSU does not seek comprehensiveness in these genres but still collects recordings by major artists, key performances, and important compositions (songs, etc.). In some instances BGSU still has greater holdings than other institutions in certain genres, however the recorded output of these genres is much too formidable to collect comprehensively.

*Third priorities* represent genres which relate only tangentially to those of the first two priorities and do not require anything but very selective representation of recordings. Many times key artists or titles cannot be identified so only samples from such genres are collected.

*Exclusions* represent that material which is not included in the collection under any circumstances. Usually another agency at the university assumes such services or collection supervision. Or, in some instances the method for carrying the sound is impractical for the library to assume or does not serve the subject needs of those genres identified as high priority.

I.  Recordings priority by format
    A. First priority
        1.  78-rpm disc (1896–ca. 1958; this speed was the primary sound carrier for popular single recordings up to about 1954, tapering off until its demise about 1958)
        2.  45-rpm disc (1949 to date; this speed was the primary sound carrier for popular single sound recordings from 1949 to the late 1980s)
        3.  33 1/3-rpm disc (1948 to date; this speed was the primary sound carrier for full length recordings from 1948 to the mid 1980s)
        4.  Compact disc recordings (early 1980s to date; this format was the secondary format up to the late 1980s but then became the primary format over the LP format by the 1990s; recordings presently owned in LP format are not currently being replaced by CD recordings, however new recordings are now being acquired on CD only)
    B. Second priority
        1.  Compact disc (key recordings already owned on LP format but representing MAJOR artists or historical compilations are being acquired here)
        2.  Cylinder (1898–1929)
    C. Third priority
        1.  8-track tape
        2.  Wire
        3.  16 2/3 rpm disc
        4.  Video cassette of music (this is a format that should be considered for inclusion in the future; the budget cannot accommodate methodical purchase at this time)

    5.  Transcription or instantaneous disc recordings
    6.  Open reel, quarter-inch audio tapes (commercial releases of very limited quantity included as samples; in-house recordings retained with old-time radio shows and the BGSU Living Archives with air shots and interviews)
    7.  Piano rolls

II.  Recordings priority by subject

    A. First priority (BGSU courses in Popular Culture, American Culture, Theatre, Speech, Music, Sociology, English, Communications, Ethnic Studies, and Applied Human Ecology)

        1.  Popular music (English language)
        2.  Rock music (English language)
        3.  Dance-orchestra, big band, disco
        4.  Rhythm and blues, soul, black urban contemporary, rap
        5.  Blues
        6.  Musicals, film music, television music
        7.  Vaudeville, burlesque, comedy, wit and humor
        8.  Jazz (styles predominant in the popular idiom, e.g., Dixieland, jazz vocals, and pre-1950s traditional)
        9.  Kiddie (e.g., mass media created stories and characterizations, presented by personalities in the popular genre)

    B. Second priority (BGSU courses in Music, Popular Culture, American Culture, Ethnic Studies, English, Speech, History, Political Science, Communication, Theatre)

        1.  Popular music (non-English language)
        2.  Rock music (non-English language)
        3.  Country, bluegrass, western swing
        4.  Gospel, spirituals, contemporary Christian, carols
        5.  Cajun, zydeco, calypso, reggae
        6.  Latino, Hispanic-American, Tex-Mex
        7.  Folk music (Anglo-American, Afro-American, and other forms existing in the United States that are influenced by foreign cultures)
        8.  Sermons
        9.  Documentary, interviews, success testimonials, and instruction
     10.  Radio shows (plays, disc jockey, etc.)
     11.  Popular dance forms (polkas, square dances, etc.)
     12.  Commercial advertising jingles, presentations, etc.
     13.  Spoken literature/English language (poetry, prose, drama)
     14.  Sound effects

C. Third priority (BGSU courses in Music, Popular Culture, American Culture, Canadian Studies)
    1. Jazz (styles predominant in the creative/non-popular idiom, e.g.: bop, third stream, avant-garde)
    2. Electronic and chance
    3. Non-pop musical forms (waltzes, marches, etc.)
D. Exclusions
    1. Classical and art music (except for 78-rpm singles and "milestone" albums)
    2. K–12 educational material
    3. Language instruction

III. Support material (non-recordings) by priority
A. First priority
    1. Major and specialized periodical titles about recordings, the record trade, and popular music forms
    2. Books on popular music and the record trade (critical monographs, discographies, biographies, historical discourses)
    3. Promotional photographs, biographical clippings, pictures, etc., on individual pop performers and groups
    4. Record company catalogs, brochures, and used record sale and auction lists
    5. LP inner sleeves and 45- and 78-rpm record outer sleeves (one example of each design change)
    6. Popular sheet music and song folios
B. Second priority
    1. Examples of record packaging and storage (storage folders, carrying cases, and racks)
    2. Record release notices
    3. Posters
C. Third priority
    1. Record promotion items (in-store stand-ups, ceiling-hanging displays, three-dimensional gimmicks, etc.)

Example 4: *Columbus Metropolitan Library, Main Library* (1994)
Note: this example of the narrative statement approach assigns codes that describe desired collection levels with additional commentary that describes current collecting intensity.

Levels of Collection Development

Level 1
Contains only materials which give an overview of a broad subject area. Selection is limited to introductory works and surveys reflecting public demand. Some purchasing is made, but no emphasis is made on a larger developed plan.

As applied to the recorded music collection, this level contains some popular recent releases, with little or no attempt to provide a balanced collection.

Level 2
Materials consist of popular or important sources which explain the major concepts of the subject areas, as well as some basic reference sources, such as encyclopedias, dictionaries, and indexes. At this level the collection would contain materials by significant authors geared specifically toward the lifestyles and aspirations of the community being served. New materials are acquired to update, not expand, the collection. In areas which are controversial, this level would endeavor to obtain at least one work which covers the two major sides of an issue.

As applied to the recorded music collection, this level contains popular recent releases, as well as a retrospective collection of materials of enduring popularity. Purchasing would be concentrated on updating the collection and adding duplicate copies to meet current demand.

Level 3
A collection which contains materials that provide balance and expanded coverage of important, subsidiary aspects of broad subjects. Materials include a broad selection of works of current interest, as well as those giving a historical overview. Also included are commentaries and other secondary sources and current subject-specific reference tools. Depth and scope of the collection may vary with new developments in the field and changing public interests. Also included will be separate works on at least two sides of major controversial issues. Retention of general works, "classics" in the field and popular titles which withstand the test of time, is the goal of this collection level.

As applied to the recorded music collection, although major emphasis will be on current popular materials, coverage will also include those with historical significance. The collection contains a broad cross-section of materials available in the field, including some lesser-known titles. Many works will be represented by several versions. Multiple copies of popular works will be purchased to meet current demands. Anticipate that Level 3 will be the optimum coverage for most major areas of the AV collection.

### Level 4

This collection level provides in-depth information on more specific aspects of the subject than does Level 3. Acquisitions include representation of the significant works in the field as well as extensive representation of significant authors. All standard reference works should be included. Indexing and abstracting services necessary to support and access the collection would be included. Local interest holdings come into play at this level. Coverage is current and retrospective. Expansion in both size and scope can be anticipated. Retention of the works of significant authors in the field and the major reference tools is a goal of this collection level. In areas which are controversial, this level would endeavor to represent all sides of a topic.

As applied to the recorded music collection, this level contains expanded historical coverage over Level 3. Significant works on a subject will be retained in the collection through continuous monitoring for needed replacements.

### Level 5

A comprehensive, in-depth collection of published source material in all formats for formal or independent study. This level includes wide selection of specialized monographs, a broad range of all important reference works, and indexing and abstracting services. Coverage is both current and retrospective. Expansion of the collection in size and scope may be anticipated. This level would retain a historical collection on all aspects of a subject including those of "popular" culture.

Anticipate little development of the recorded music collection at this level. An example of a Level 5 music collection would include samples of all artists in a particular genre.

### Level 6

A collection which contains all available material on the subject in all appropriate formats.

Anticipate no development of the recorded music collection at this level. An example of a Level 6 music collection would include all works of every recording artist in a particular genre.

MUSIC CLASSIFICATION

The Main Library recorded music collection is primarily arranged according to the *ANSCR* classification system. An abbreviated form of *ANSCR* is utilized for shelving and display purposes. In some areas *ANSCR* does not reflect collection needs or current trends in the recording industry. As a result, some materials have been pulled out of the *ANSCR* scheme and are considered separately.

A    MUSIC HISTORY

This section includes recordings which provide instruction or some other form of music history. In general items of this sort can be given Dewey classifications and shelved with nonfiction audio. Since there are only a few items in the "A" classification, this section may be phased out. Early music and Gregorian chant, which used to be in this section, are now kept in chamber music (F), vocal music (D), or choral music (C) depending on the nature of the performance.

B    OPERA                                    DL=4

Operas are musical dramatic works in which the actors sing some of their parts usually accompanied by instruments or an orchestra. Operas combine music, drama, and spectacle. Beginning in the seventeenth century, the development of opera has involved various stages including *tragédie lyrique* in France, *opera seria* in Italy, comic opera in England, *Singspiel* in Germany, and others.

All major and some minor works by important opera composers and a sample of operas by other composers will be selected. Operas by contemporary composers will also be included in the collection. Multiple performances by different singers and conductors of popular operas will be selected.

The collection will also include operettas as well as collections of arias and duets performed by well-known singers. Excerpts from operas and opera choruses will also be sampled. Many operas are also available on video (782.1).

C    CHORAL MUSIC                            DL=3

This section includes music written for a chorus of multiple voices, that is with more than one singer per part. It may be monophonic, as in Gregorian chant, or polyphonic (more than one independent voice). There may or may not be instrumental accompaniment or additional solo vocal parts. Choruses may be male, female, or mixed voices and may be only a few voices or over a hundred. Principal choral forms include anthems, cantatas, chorales, hymns, masses, motets, oratorios, passions, and Te Deums. Works which are appropriate for specific holidays will be included. In addition to these religious forms, there is also a smaller repertoire of secular choral music.

This section also includes choirs performing choral arrangements of popular or patriotic music.

D     VOCAL MUSIC                           DL=3

This section is for solo voice or vocal duets, trios, quartets, in which there is one voice per part. It may be a cappella or accompanied by piano or other instrument or by an instrumental ensemble. Repertoire includes art songs, lieder, song cycles, and earlier forms such as solo cantatas, chansons, airs, laude, cantigas, as well as the early music of minnesingers and troubadours. The collection includes recordings of recitals by well-known singers. Also included are performances of spirituals and parlor songs by classically trained singers. American and contemporary art songs will also be included in the collection.

EA     ORCHESTRAL MUSIC                     DL=4

The orchestra is "an organized body of bowed strings, with more than one player to a part, to which may be added wind and percussion instruments" (*The Norton/Grove Concise Encyclopedia of Music*, 541). This section includes all orchestral recordings except symphonies, concertos, and ballet music. Forms include overtures, suites, symphonic poems, variations, preludes, orchestral excerpts from operas, orchestra marches, and others.

The collection will include multiple performances of the major repertoire and a sampling of lesser-known pieces. Orchestral works by American and contemporary composers will also be represented. Examples of all the major conductors and orchestras will be included.

EB     BALLET MUSIC                         DL=3

This section includes music written or adapted for the staged performance of dance, either ballet or modern dance. The collection will include various versions of the major ballets and a sampling of other lesser-known works.

EC     CONCERTOS                            DL=4

Concertos include music contrasting a solo instrument or instruments with the orchestral ensemble. The concerto is one of the major forms of classical music which has been developed by many composers featuring almost every instrument. The collection includes concertos by all major composers as well as those less well-known. Major works will include multiple versions by different artists, and performances by well-known soloists will be emphasized.

ES   SYMPHONIES                          DL=4

The symphony is an extended work for orchestra usually in three or four sections. The collection will include multiple interpretations of the major symphonic works along with a sampling of symphonies by more obscure composers. Symphonies by American composers and contemporary symphonies will also be selected. Examples of all the major conductors and orchestras will be included.

F    CHAMBER MUSIC                       DL=4

Chamber music includes "music for small ensembles of solo instruments, written for performance under domestic circumstances in a drawing-room or small hall . . ." (*New Grove* 4:113); by this definition "chamber music" could include solo instrumental music or even vocals with a small instrumental group. The library uses the *ANSCR* definition of chamber music, which is narrower: "music . . . performed by instrumental groups of not less than three nor more than nine instruments, and in which only one player is assigned to each part." Not included are chamber orchestras (EA), string ensembles (EA), or wind ensembles (H) of more than nine instruments. Solo instruments (e.g., piano solos = GP) or solos with accompaniment (e.g., violin sonatas = GV) are a different category.

Chamber music includes trio sonatas, string quartets, string trios, piano trios, piano quartets, piano quintets, string quintets, wind quartets or quintets, septets, string sextets, octets, nonets, and other combinations. The collection includes the basic works by the best known composers, selections by well-known artists, and a sampling of other composers and performing groups.

GG   GUITAR MUSIC                        DL=3

This section includes music for guitar or guitar duets, trios and larger ensembles. Also included is solo or duet music for lute, mandolin and other similar instruments. The repertoire includes pieces written for the guitar as well as many transcriptions. The lute and mandolin have smaller repertoires which are sampled. Guitar music has an audience beyond the "classical" field, appealing to the "new age" and "Spanish/flamenco" listener. However, "new age" guitar music is shelved with other "new age" music, and flamenco guitar is shelved with international music (Q).

GO   ORGAN MUSIC                         DL=3

This section features music for the pipe organ or electronic variants. There is a large repertoire of pieces including preludes, fugues, toccatas, and chorales. Representative selections by important composers as well as collections by significant organists will be collected.

### GP   PIANO MUSIC                         DL=4

This section includes solo piano, piano duets, piano choirs, as well as harpsichord, clavichord, and other similar keyboard instruments. There is a large repertoire of piano music, including sonatas, variations, character pieces, transcriptions, rags, and light parlor pieces. There are also many well-known soloists whose recordings will be selected.

### GS   STRING INSTRUMENTS               DL=3

String instruments include viola, cello, double bass, harp, viol, and other historical instruments. This section includes music for solo string instruments (except the violin) and solo string instruments accompanied by a piano or other instrument. It also includes duets. Concertos are not included but collections of encores, which might include orchestral accompaniment, are included. There is a fairly extensive cello repertoire and a number of well-known soloists who are to be represented. The other instruments have smaller repertoires which will be sampled.

### GV   VIOLIN MUSIC                       DL=3

This section includes music for solo violin and music for violin accompanied by piano or continuo (harpsichord plus viol). It also includes duets. Concertos are not included, but collections of encores, which might include orchestral accompaniment, are included. The violin has a large repertoire and there are many well-known soloists who will continue to be selected.

### GW   WIND INSTRUMENTS                  DL=2

Wind instruments include woodwinds (flute, recorder, clarinet, oboe, English horn, bassoon, and saxophone) and brass instruments (trumpet, trombone, French horn, tuba). This section includes music for solo wind instruments or a wind instrument with accompaniment by piano or another instrument. Duets are also included. Concertos are not included but collections of encores, which might include orchestral accompaniment, are included. There is a large repertoire for solo flute, and a fairly large repertoire for solo clarinet and trumpet. Interest in other solo woodwinds is growing and a core selection for each instrument is desired.

GX   PERCUSSION INSTRUMENTS          DL=2
Percussion music uses instruments which are "played by shaking, or by striking a membrane or a plate or bar of metal, wood, or other hard material." (*The Norton/Grove Concise Encyclopedia of Music*, 567). Some instruments sound a definite pitch and others do not. Instruments include various drums, cymbals, xylophones, bells, chimes, carillon, gongs, tambourines, wood blocks, and many others. This category includes music for solo percussion and percussion ensembles. This section also incorporates unusual instruments such as the glass harmonica. It is a specialized area with a limited repertoire and a fairly small number of available recordings.

H   BAND MUSIC                               DL=3
This section includes marching bands, brass bands, fife and drum units, drum and bugle corps, bagpipe bands, concert or symphonic bands, and wind ensembles of more than nine instruments. Groups may or may not include percussion instruments. Also included may be college fight songs and patriotic music. Collections which reflect United States history will be selected.

J   ELECTRONIC MUSIC                    DL=2
Electronic music uses electronic means to create music or modify existing sounds. Historically it includes the theremin (1920s), ondes martenot, and analog and digital synthesizers. It also includes *musique concrète* and other music in which tape recorders or computers are used to manipulate pre-existing or synthesized sounds. It does not include popular music using electric instruments or synthesizers, although purely instrumental synthesizer music would be included. This category also includes mechanical instruments such as the musical clock, barrel organ, music box, and player piano. It is a fairly specialized area with a few well-known composers and many lesser-known experimenters.
Original electronic music has a relatively small audience but transcriptions of classical pieces for synthesizer have been popular. Collections of important historical works and a sampling of popular transcriptions and new works are selected.

K   MUSICAL SHOWS                        DL=4
Musical shows are defined as plays embellished with songs. The story line can be dramatic, comic, tragic, or any combination of these three. The music can be any type or style that is considered as popular music. Sound recordings of musicals offer the unique experience of evoking the emotions of the original performance.
Revues, which do not use a story line, but instead compile short farcical or satirical sketches, are an important part of this art form. This

section also includes collections of songs from musicals. There is also some crossover with musical soundtracks. Programs originally produced on stage may be filmed, often with an entirely different cast. (Any made-for-film version will be shelved with soundtracks.)

Collection development centers around well-known writers, performers, and Tony Award winning shows. Particular emphasis is given to obtaining multiple copies (three to five) of shows appearing locally.

The collection includes performances both by original casts and successful revivals. Diversity will be sought through representation of productions by ethnic casts. Shows that are considered standards of American theater and music will be closely monitored for replacement as necessary.

L　　SOUNDTRACKS　　　　　　　　　DL=3

For the purpose of this collection, soundtracks are defined as music written or arranged for motion pictures, video tapes, television programs, or commercials. The time period covered is from the early 1920s to date.

Movie soundtracks often cross over into current popular music, adding a level of appreciation apart from the film itself. The soundtrack can become an experience which stands apart from the film.

Collection development is based heavily on Oscar/Grammy Award winning shows and on films appearing in local screenings.

This collection has some crossover titles with musicals. Titles originally produced on stage may be filmed, often with an entirely different cast and new songs added.

MA　POPULAR MUSIC　　　　　　　　　DL=3

Popular music is a term used to refer to music that is accessible to and enjoyed by the general public, as distinguished from music intended for a more musically sophisticated or experienced listener. Popular music for this division is defined as contemporary music produced during the years 1960 to present; this range of years will change as time passes. This category includes contemporary interpretations of Tin Pan Alley standards as well as newer songs in similar styles. The term usually excludes classical, folk, jazz, rock, gospel, country, Broadway shows, and movie soundtracks. Isolated works from any of these genres may become popular music, however, through a different version or artist. There is also a great deal of crossover, with artists whose major volume of work is in another category occasionally producing popular music.

The collection will sample the work of all significant artists and provide more in-depth holdings of artists of recognized importance.

Instrumental versions of popular standards will be purchased when available.

### NOSTALGIA & BIG BAND    DL=4

This collection includes popular American music produced between 1890 and 1960. Specific types of music covered are the Big Band era, the World War I and II eras, the pre-rock 'n' roll fifties, ragtime (also found in Piano Music = GP), barbershop quartets, and the work of artists who came to prominence within this time period. Types of music *not* included here are Broadway shows, movie soundtracks, rock, gospel, country, and the work of artists from this time period produced since 1960.

It should be noted that Nostalgia and Big Band is not a recognized *ANSCR* category but was created by this division in response to customer demand for these materials.

A great deal of emphasis has been placed on obtaining collections with a variety of performers to insure the fullest possible coverage of time periods, and to include the work of artists that may be unavailable in any other form.

The level reflects a commitment to monitor and replace items as needed in order to ensure historical coverage of important American materials.

### MC   COUNTRY MUSIC                DL=4

Country is a type of popular music that originated in the southern and western region of the United States, though it has become more widespread in recent years. It is derived from rural folk music, which in turn was derived from folk music of the British Isles brought to this country by immigrants. This genre of regional folk music has continued to evolve, becoming part of the mainstream popular culture. The local area music scene is a part of the evolution. Columbus has a large segment of population with an Appalachian heritage, and this has had a significant effect in terms of music heard on local radio stations and performers who regularly appear here.

Country includes old time music, bluegrass, western swing, cowboy songs, and honky tonk, and is influenced by religious and traditional African American styles. There is also some overlap with other contemporary styles.

Country has a long tradition of songs with vocals that tell a story, as well as purely instrumental recordings. The primary instruments are strings—fiddle, guitar, steel guitar, banjo, and mandolin, sometimes accompanied by piano and drums.

The division has a commitment to maintain a collection of historical standards, as well as recent works by established artists and by new and upcoming musicians. The different styles represented by Nashville, Tennessee; Austin, Texas; and Bakersfield, California will be represented. This will be accomplished by ordering and to some extent replacing works by major artists in the genre, and by obtaining historical and contemporary anthologies. Attention will also be given to recordings by local artists.

## MG   GOSPEL                          DL=3

This section includes various kinds of popular religious music, including popular recordings of hymns and spirituals, African American gospel styles (soloists, quartets, and mass choirs), inspirational recordings, and contemporary Christian music.

Recordings of spirituals and anthems by classical singers or choirs are included in the classical choral (C) or vocal (D) sections, along with religious works in the Western European tradition such as the requiem or mass.

The collection will include representative recordings by significant historical artists. Anthologies which represent various time periods or styles will also be included. A selection of recordings by contemporary artists will be included based on popularity and demand. This area is one which is in a growth and developmental stage and emphasis will be on obtaining new recordings by a variety of artists while retaining classic historical performances.

## MJ   JAZZ                            DL=4

Jazz is an American musical style which began in African American urban communities around the turn of the century and has developed a variety of styles which are now played and listened to around the world. Jazz is characterized by the improvised solo; therefore, recordings are the major documentation of its history. Along with live performances (sometimes limited to a few large cities), recordings are the primary means of its dissemination today.

Major stylistic genres in jazz include New Orleans, Chicago, Dixieland, swing, bebop, cool, hard bop, free jazz, fusion, and third stream. Blues and ragtime both influenced jazz but are not part of jazz. Jazz may be performed by any size group, but the trio, combo (four to seven players), and the big band are the most common. Instruments include trumpet, clarinet, trombone, or saxophone as soloists, or in sections (big bands), supported by a rhythm section of piano, bass (acoustic or electric), sometimes guitar, and the drum kit.

The collection will maintain the significant recordings by major artists in all jazz genres, as well as a selection of recordings by other artists in a variety of styles. This will require ordering and selectively replacing works by major artists in the genre, and obtaining historical anthologies of major styles and historical periods. Recordings of contemporary artists in all styles will be selected based on popularity, demand, and reviewing sources. Attention will also be given to recordings by local artists.

### NEW AGE MUSIC  DL=3
"The term 'New Age music' does not refer to any specific genre of music; rather, it refers to music that is used therapeutically or for other New Age (and inherently nonmusical) purposes" (*New Age Encyclopedia*); in record stores it is a marketing slogan rather than a musical category; its purposes may include providing background, relaxation, meditation, healing, or achieving altered consciousness.

Although its history is very brief (not much beyond ten years), there are certain recognized new age performers. There are also certain record labels which specialize in new age music.

Recognizable new age styles include East/West, Electronic/Computer, New Acoustic Folk, Jazz/Fusion, Meditation Music, Native American, Progressive, Solo Instrumental, Sound Health Music, Space Music, and World Music. The related genre, Minimalism, is kept in the appropriate classical music section. Related areas in other parts of the collection include environmental recordings (Y), electronic music (J), relaxation music (100s), jazz (MJ), folk music (P), world music (Q), chamber music (F), solo piano (GP), and solo guitar (GG). New items in these areas which would be of interest to new age listeners will be considered for selection.

The collection will include significant recordings by major performers as well as a selection of recordings by other performers in each new age area and anthologies representing the various recording labels. As a new area for development, selection of new age recordings will emphasize obtaining most new releases on recognized labels in a range of styles and retention of works by popular performers. Recordings will be selected based on popularity, demand, and reviewing sources.

### BLUES  DL=3
Blues is an African American music which began around 1900 in the rural areas of the south and has continued to develop in both rural and urban areas. Its influence on other forms of popular music, including rock and country music, has been significant.

Styles include rural down-home blues, vaudeville or classic blues, city blues, modern blues, and blues-rock. There have been many regional styles, including Mississippi Delta blues, Chicago blues, Texas blues, and Piedmont blues. In addition to a variety of vocal techniques, blues features unique styles on guitar, piano, and harmonica.

The collection will include significant recordings by major artists as well as a selection of recordings by other artists. While an attempt will be made to sample the work of many artists, it is not feasible to collect complete works for all but the most significant artists. Anthologies which focus on a particular region or style will be emphasized for their educational value. Recordings of contemporary artists will be selected based on popularity, demand, and reviewing sources.

MR    ROCK MUSIC                        DL=3

Rock is a type of American popular music that developed out of rock 'n' roll, which is in the rock oldies section. The MR section also includes rhythm and blues and soul produced since 1971. The current stage of rock uses amplified singing and electric instruments, including primarily lead, rhythm, and bass guitars, drums, keyboards, and synthesizers. The music often has a strong rhythmic drive intended to encourage listeners to dance. The lyrics mainly deal with subjects of interest to young adults. There is a lot of cross-generational interest in this category—people from the baby boomer generation who are now in their forties, as well as teenagers and young adults. The music itself is of primary importance in rock, especially as performed by the "guitar hero." In terms of our collection, MR is defined as rock music produced since 1971. The range of years included will change as time and styles change.

Since its beginning, rock has always been the music of the young and often expresses their feeling of revolution against all that has gone before—in terms of music in particular and society in general.

Rock has become subdivided into many categories—folk rock, hard rock, art rock—and within recent years new styles are appearing almost yearly, such as heavy metal, punk, new wave, thrash, grunge, and rap, to name only a few.

The collection will always include a representative sampling of popular artists from the styles and time period covered, but there will be no effort to develop or maintain a comprehensive collection. Some replacement of titles will be made based on customer requests and for reserve requests from branches.

The library does not label any music regarding content, but we also do not remove labels put on by record companies. Some materials may be controversial in nature, but since they are not selected for children, they are considered adult material. The library has a commitment to purchase and maintain a representative sampling of the music that is available on open airwaves and for purchase in record stores. Attention will also be given to recordings by local artists.

ROCK OLDIES                          DL=4

The rock oldies section covers popular music produced during the years 1950–1971. Types of music included in this category are: rockabilly, rock 'n' roll, rock, rhythm & blues, and soul. Types of music specifically NOT included here are: jazz, blues, country, gospel, folk, Broadway shows, and movie soundtracks. The range of years covered will change as time and styles change.

Society in general, and popular music in particular, underwent a great deal of change in the 1950s and 1960s. This is reflected in the range of artists included here.

This collection includes a number of anthologies to ensure the fullest possible coverage of the time period and to include the works of artists that may be unavailable in any other form. The collection will be regularly monitored, since the division has a commitment to replace items as needed.

As with Nostalgia & Big Band, Rock Oldies is not a recognized *ANSCR* category but was created by this division in response to customer demand.

P     U.S. FOLK MUSIC                DL=3

This area includes three types of music: traditional American folk music, music of the urban folk revival, and regional music of ethnic groups in the United States. Traditional folk music in the United States includes a wide variety of genres including fiddle and dance tunes, cowboy songs, topical and love ballads, and religious folk tunes. Collections of field recordings from various regions of the country as well as active traditional performers will be selected.

Urban folk music began in the 1930s and continued with the folk revival of the 1960s. Significant performers from this movement as well as contemporary performers in this tradition will be selected. Anthologies which represent a historical overview will be emphasized.

The desire for a diverse multicultural collection makes the music of the many ethnic groups in the United States including Hispanic American, Native American, European American, and Asian American groups an important area for growth. The genres of ethnic music which are currently being developed include the French-Louisiana styles, Cajun and zydeco; the Hispanic Tex-Mex of the Southwestern states; Hawaiian music; and European American polkas. Latin music and salsa, as well as Yiddish American and klezmer music, are shelved with international music. Music of other ethnic groups may also be developed in the future depending on demand and availability of recordings.

Anthologies which present a variety of performers in these genres will be emphasized as well as a selection of recordings by significant artists and a sampling of newer performers. Recordings of contemporary artists will be selected based on popularity, demand, and reviewing sources.

### Q     INTERNATIONAL MUSIC          DL=3

This section includes popular and folk music from outside the United States. It includes music from every inhabited continent: Africa, Asia, North, South, and Central America, the Caribbean, Europe, the Middle East, Australia and Oceania. Music will be in many languages (including English). This area also includes Latin and salsa music and Yiddish and klezmer music. Reggae is in its own section. A collection of national anthems for as many countries as is feasible will be maintained.

The collection will include music by current artists with established popularity as well as recordings of folk music from many diverse cultures. Anthologies which give a balanced picture of the music of a culture will be emphasized. With the growth of Columbus's international community and a general increase in interest in music from other cultures, this will be a growth area of the collection. While an attempt will be made to obtain the music of as many countries and cultures as is practical, there will always be limits based on space considerations and the irregular distribution of some world music. Recordings of contemporary artists will be selected based on popularity, demand, reviewing sources, and availability.

### REGGAE                          DL=2

Reggae is a form of Jamaican popular music which has become known around the world since the 1970s. Its history includes the earlier styles: mento, ska, bluebeat, and rock steady. Performers from Africa and other countries who have also developed reggae styles will be included, but the many popular music groups who have included reggae within their own styles will not be included here. The reggae collection is a unique part of the international collection because of its wide crossover into popular music.

The collection will include significant recordings by major performers as well as a selection of recordings by other artists. Anthologies representing various styles will also be selected. Regular replacement of classic recordings by popular artists due to heavy use and loss or damage will be necessary. Recordings of contemporary artists will be selected based on popularity, demand, availability, and reviewing sources.

### R     HOLIDAY MUSIC

For the purpose of this statement, holiday music is split into two groups:

CHRISTMAS MUSIC          DL=3

SPECIAL HOLIDAY          DL=2
HALLOWEEN
HANUKKAH
EASTER
PASSOVER

Christmas music includes traditional and recent popular releases. Comedy albums, parodies, and genre-oriented collections such as jazz, blues, rock, and country style music are also included. Great emphasis is given to the purchase of multiple copies (three to ten) in an effort to meet seasonal demand.

Some music appropriate for Christmas is shelved in classical and other sections.

Collection development for special holidays is limited to availability. As with Christmas music, great emphasis is given to obtaining multiple copies (five to ten) in an effort to fill seasonal demand. Halloween music may also include appropriate sound effects. As collections of music become available for additional holidays, they will be added to this area.

WEDDING                  DL=3

Wedding music is not officially cataloged in this area, but has been pulled from throughout the collection. Most recordings are selections of vocal or organ arrangements of traditional wedding music. More collections of popular love songs that have been commonly used at weddings over the past few decades are currently being added. Additional music appropriate for weddings may also be shelved with popular or classical music. Multiple copies (five to ten) of representative titles are needed.

S   VARIETIES AND HUMOR      DL=0
T   PLAYS                    DL=0
U   POETRY                   DL=0
V   PROSE                    DL=0
W   DOCUMENTARY              DL=0
X   INSTRUCTIONAL            DL=0

Materials formerly classed in these *ANSCR* categories are now included in nonfiction books-on-tape. Materials from these categories in audiocassette format have been reclassed with Dewey numbers, and those in record format have been ordered in ac/cd where necessary. They will be classed in nonfiction when received.

Y    SOUND EFFECTS                    DL=3

This category includes two distinct types of sound effects: human-mechanical and environmental. Human-mechanical sound effects include groups of short recordings (seconds/minutes) of all types of machines, music effects, crowd sounds, and human sounds. The purpose of these recordings is to provide a specific background sound effect. Collections appropriate for Halloween may be here or in Holiday Music (R).

Environmental sound effects include groups of short recordings of individually named birds and animals, for wildlife identification, as well as longer recordings of natural ambiance—waves on the seashore, rainfall, forest and jungle sounds as a whole.

Growth centers on identifying gaps in the collection, replacement of lost/damaged materials, and finding quality products available in the marketplace.

# 3

# Middlebury College Music Library
# Collection Development Policy

January 17, 1994

I. Introduction

A. Purpose

This policy outlines in a detailed form the principles of collection development that are defined by the Music Library and is a supplement to the Egbert Starr Library Collection Development Policy. Collection policy is coordinated with the special collections residing in the Flanders Ballad Collection and the Vermont Archives of Traditional Music. Only areas that differ or expand on the latter will be addressed in the Music Library policy. The policy communicates the collection policies and goals of the library to library users and librarians. The document is to be used as the basis for decision making for the selection of individual items for the collection and for the allocation of funds. It also informs librarians in the processes of deselection and collection evaluation.

B. Institution and Clientele

Middlebury College is an undergraduate liberal arts institution with an intensive study program in foreign languages operating in the summer. The music department offers the B.A. degree. The Summer Language Schools and the Breadloaf School of English offer advanced degrees. The library serves four principal groups: students, faculty, staff, and the greater community. These groups have differing, yet overlapping, needs for library materials and service in the area of music. Some of these needs as they relate to music are: study and instruction, performance and composition, research and information, cultural and aesthetic enlightenment, and entertainment and recreation.

The library's primary clientele is undergraduate liberal arts students whose needs encompass all of the categories enumerated above but with an emphasis on study, performance, composition, and research. Among the undergraduate students, the library serves both music majors and non-majors. The music major has the opportunity to explore virtually any aspect of music, but the department emphasizes composition, performance, ethnomusicology, and music history and theory. Courses for the non-major are generally introductory in nature and serve to fulfill the broad educational needs of the liberal arts curriculum. In addition, the institution has a strong interest in promoting interdisciplinary studies.

Students at the Summer Language Schools may use music to complement their study of a language at the undergraduate level. Summer language offerings at the graduate level sometimes focus on a musical topic as a means of advanced instruction in the culture associated with a particular language.

The Middlebury College faculty members are chosen for their excellence as teachers and scholars. Teaching is considered the primary responsibility of the faculty. Faculty research is intended to enhance the teaching mission of the institution and the faculty.

The library's collection is also available as a resource to college staff and the Middlebury community. These groups are important to the college community and are encouraged to make use of the music library collection which is primarily designed to serve the instructional needs of students.

C. Mission and Goals

It is the mission of the Music Library collection development and management program to select and maintain a collection of library materials related to the instructional, research, intellectual and artistic interests of students and faculty.

1. To acquire all library materials necessary for instructional purposes.
2. To acquire research materials to support teaching.
3. To develop a strong reference collection designed to assist individuals in locating materials necessary for their research and information needs and to prepare students who may continue with graduate work in music.
4. To develop a collection of performance materials for all vocal ranges and for each instrument of the orchestra including chamber works, but excluding collections of parts for large ensembles.
5. To develop a music collection in various formats that fulfills human needs for artistic expression and recreation including a representation of popular music.
6. To acquire music materials that will enhance the study of foreign languages and cultures represented in the Middlebury College curriculum.

D. Intellectual Freedom and Censorship

The Music Library will observe and apply to music materials the principles outlined in *The Freedom to Read* statement, the *Library Bill of Rights*, the *Intellectual Freedom Statement*, and supporting documents as appended to the Egbert Starr Library Collection Development Policy.

E. Overview of the Collection

1. History of the Collection

The Music Library collection was developed both by Starr Library and the Music Department with the Library being responsible for acquiring books, periodicals, and study scores and the Department acquiring recordings and performance materials. With the construction of the Christian A. Johnson Building and the growing recognition of the Department for the need of greater library resources and a librarian to administer those resources, the Music Library developed into a branch library in 1971-1972 where all of the scores, recordings, reference books, and current periodicals were kept. In 1992 the Music Library moved to the Center for the Arts where all library materials relating to music were brought together for the first time.

The collection has grown significantly over the last twenty-five years from a small departmental collection to a library offering a full range of services to the entire College community. The Music Library has taken advantage of new technologies as they emerge. This has led to the collection of a wide variety of library materials in various formats, including books, periodicals, microforms, printed music, sound recordings (LPs, CDs, cassettes), video recordings (VHS cassettes and laser discs), and computer software (floppy discs and CD-ROMs).

The collection has always existed to support curricular offerings at the College, but there have also been special programs that influenced collecting in certain areas not immediately reflected in the curriculum. The Composer's Conference & Chamber Music Center was started in 1945 and was run by Alan Carter, chairman of the College Music Department. The Composer's Conference & Chamber Music Center used the department's chamber music collection throughout the years, and the Music Library was involved in the administration of the program from 1971 to 1983. The program then moved to Wellesley College. During this period the Music Library acquired a representative collection of chamber music, including multiple copies of parts of works from the standard repertory.

The Flanders Ballads Collection came to Middlebury College in 1941 and was actively maintained through 1960. Over the next fifteen years, little attention was given to the archive that was housed in Starr Library. Renewed interest rescued the materials from neglect beginning in 1975. Work on expanding the collection was recognized in 1986 with the establishment of the Vermont Archives of Traditional Music under the curatorship of Jennifer Post. The two collections were moved in 1992 to the Center for the Arts and are administered separately from the Music Library. These two collections are the college's most important special collections in music and are known nationally and internationally for their unique contribution to our under-standing of folk music in New England.

The Special Collections Department of Starr Library also contains some materials on music including a thirteenth-century gradual, some nineteenth-century music imprints, and twentieth-century first editions of music. The College Archives maintains the documents of the Music Department.

2. Areas of Emphasis

The Music Library collection maintains a strong core collection in the history and theory of Western music. For an institution of its size, it has developed a strong collection of the monuments of music and collected works of composers. The Music Library maintains a commitment to this area of emphasis.

Other emphases have changed over the years as curricular offerings reflected the unique talents and expertise of the college's music faculty or have been influenced by institutional programs and policies. Some recent areas of interest have been: American music, twentieth-century music, music by women composers, musical composition, jazz, opera, and ethnomusicology. The Music Library will support the emphases of the music curriculum through the introductory study level.

3. Collection Locations
Library resources in music are located in the Music Library. Music materials may also be located in various special collections if it is important to maintain the provenance of the material in the collection.

F. Organization of Collection Management and Development Program
1. Staffing
The music librarian has the principal responsibility for the determination and implementation of the program. Collection policies are created through consultation with the music faculty and the collection development librarian. Decisions related to special materials are coordinated with the Abernethy Curator and Archivist, and the Curator of the Flanders Ballads Collection and Vermont Archives of Traditional Music.

The collection policies for books, serials, and microforms are jointly administered by the collection development librarian and the music librarian. The acquisition of serials is subject to review by the Serials Review Committee. The acquisition of materials in all other formats collected by the Music Library is directly administered by the music librarian.

2. Liaison with User Groups
The music librarian is responsible for maintaining a close working relationship with the music faculty to ensure that current collection policies result in selection decisions that adequately reflect curricular offerings. The music librarian is also responsive to collection needs as perceived by faculty and students in other departments. Active solicitation of other user groups will generally not

be undertaken as it falls outside the mission of the Music Library.

G. Relationship to Other Policies

The collection development policy must be reviewed in light of related library policies as they currently exist and/or are developed, such as: Starr Library, Flanders Collection, Vermont Archives of Traditional Music, and Special Collections collection development policies; gifts policy statement; circulation, interlibrary loan, preservation, replacement, and deselection policies.

H. Cooperative Collection Development Agreements

Because Middlebury College is a residential college and is geographically isolated from other academic or research collections, it is important to develop a strong library collection, to make appropriate use of interlibrary loan, and to take advantage of future technological developments that will increase access to music library materials. For these reasons cooperative collection development agreements will not be pursued.

II. General Collection Management and Development Policies

A. Format of Material

1. Books

The Music Library adheres to the extensive guidelines enumerated in the Starr Library Collection Development Policy. Emphasis in that document is given to material of lasting and scholarly value.

2. Periodicals

The Music Library follows the Starr Library Collection Development Policy (section L) regarding serials. The Serials Review Committee will apply those guidelines to recommendations made by the Music Library and Department Faculty in determining appropriate titles for the collection.

3. Newspapers

Newspaper subscriptions are subject to review by the Serials Review Committee. In general, the Music Library will recommend acquiring one major national newspaper and one local newspaper in order to have current reporting on musical and other cultural events.

4. Textbooks

Because the Music Department offers introductory courses to a large number of students, textbooks will be acquired with more frequency than for the general library collection. Nonetheless, the selection guidelines for exceptions in the Starr Library Collection Development Policy (section N) will be followed. The library collects textbooks used in all Music Department courses.

5. Reprints and Reissues

Reprinted books and music are acquired when needed if there is not a work available representing current scholarly opinion on a subject or a recently prepared edition. Reprints will also be selected for works that are considered major studies in their time and whose content has not been totally superseded by more recent studies.

No distinction will be made between recent and reissued recordings and visual materials. The selection decision will be made solely upon the content and quality of the performance.

6. Dissertations and Theses

Generally not acquired. See Starr Library Collection Development Policy (section E).

7. Paperbacks

See Starr Library Collection Development Policy (section F, paragraph 2).

8. Microforms

See Starr Library Collection Development Policy (section I).

9. Pamphlets and Newsletters

These materials are acquired if they are free and are related to some aspect of the curriculum. They are located in the vertical files. Catalogs from publishers, recording companies, instrument manufacturers, and audio equipment are retained for no longer than five years.

10. Printed Music

a. Reference scores

Priority will be given to acquiring sets of the complete works of the major composers from all periods of Western music history. Secondarily, the Music Library will acquire major sets and series related to the music of a particular country, region, or historical time period. These sets will be collected much more sparingly. These series will be chosen based on the projected content of the series which must contain literature by significant composers of the country or time or, in the case of early music, must publish the contents of an important manuscript collection. Selection of these sets will be guided by their citation in standard music histories or by the textbook used for teaching music history at the college.

Due to the expensive nature of these materials, the Music Library will attempt to allocate no more than half of its budget for printed music for these resources.

b. Facsimiles and Microforms

Facsimiles of manuscripts are acquired only at the direct request of a music faculty member to support classroom instruction. The facsimile should adhere to the highest standards of facsimile reproduction including faithfulness to the original colors, size (or clearly indicate the reduction ratio), and text. It should also be accompanied with appropriate scholarly analysis of the manuscript and explanation of the techniques used in producing the facsimile. In no case will the library acquire facsimiles that have been "touched-up" editorially to "improve" the text.

Microforms of music are acquired only at the direct request of a music faculty member to support classroom instruction. (See section I. Microforms of the Starr Library Collection Development Policy.)

These criteria will not apply to editions of contemporary compositions that are published only in facsimile. The criteria for acquiring printed scores and parts will apply to these works.

c. Study and Miniature Scores

Scores of music with reduced prints will be acquired for study purposes in preference to a full score if the cost of the full score is one-third or more greater than the cost of the study score. Study scores will also be selected in preference to full scores if, in the judgment of the selector, it is a work that is unlikely to be performed at the college because of the size of the performing forces required or technical difficulty (e.g., full-scale operas).

d. Urtext Performance Editions

All new urtext editions will be acquired. If the library already has an urtext edition published within the last ten years by another publisher, the work will not be acquired unless review literature indicates that significantly new material or scholarly interpretation is represented by the newer edition.

e. Performance Editions

The library will acquire performance editions for instrumental and vocal literature proportionate to the current enrollment in the applied music program. Preference will be given to editions having scores and parts over editions of parts only.

Preference will also be given to works in their original instrumentation over arrangements. Arrangements by the composer or authorized by the composer, works arranged by another major composer, or well-known arrangements may be standard exceptions. Concertos and solos for an instrument and large ensemble will be acquired in arrangements for solo instrument and keyboard.

f. Vocal Scores

Vocal scores of major works and composers of operas, operettas, musicals, revues, oratorios, cantatas, orchestra songs, and songs with instrumental accompaniment are collected. Preference is given to selecting editions of the complete work over editions of selected arias or songs from a work. (See also section II. C. Languages and translations.)

g. Vocal Ensemble Music

Scores of vocal ensemble music by major composers, both accompanied and a cappella, are collected. (See also sections II.C. Languages and translations and II. F. Multiple copies.)

h. Works for Large Ensembles

Performance materials for ensembles requiring more than ten performers will not be collected by the Music Library but may be acquired for the orchestra, band, or choral libraries by the music department.

i. Pedagogical Materials

A selection of music intended for instructional purposes, including etudes, orchestral excerpts, and technical studies (e.g., scales), will be acquired for all of the instruments of the orchestra, harpsichord, organ, piano, guitar, and for voice. Other instructional material will be acquired as dictated by the demands of the applied program (e.g., jazz studies, early instruments).

j. Choice of Edition

The library will select editions whenever possible that represent careful scholarly editing techniques. Performance editions prepared by a major performer will be selected if the edition serves to document the performance practice of the period in which the piece was composed or is historically significant in some other respect. The library will not select low cost editions simply to fill in gaps in the repertory or to expand the holdings of the library quickly.

11. Sound Recordings

The library acquires compact discs (CDs), vinyl discs (LPs), and cassettes in that order of preference. The Library does not collect 78-rpm recordings or any recording formats developed prior to 331/3-rpm recordings. The library maintains an archival collection of recordings on open reel tape and cassette of musical events recorded at Middlebury College. In general, the library is not a sound recording archive and may replace recordings in older formats with identical recorded performances in newer formats as funds permit.

A decision to change format preference or to add another recording format to the collection will be based upon (in this order of importance):

1. the general commercial availability of titles required by the Library
2. the cost of the playback equipment and the format are not prohibitively expensive
3. the obsolescence of a currently acquired format
4. the ability to interface with computer technology for enhanced instructional possibilities or other technological advances
5. the durability of the format and its suitability as a long-term storage medium
6. compact size

The library collects only musical sound recordings. Spoken word, sound effects, sounds of nature, etc., are not within the scope of the collection.

12. Video Recordings

The library collects laser discs and VHS video cassettes and in that order of preference. The criteria for evaluating format additions and changes follows the points listed under sound recordings (see section II.A.11. paragraph 2). In the case of motion pictures transferred to video, letterbox editions will be acquired whenever possible.

The collection will emphasize musical dramatic productions where the visual content is important and significant for a full appreciation of the artistic work. Video recordings of concerts will be collected very selectively using these criteria: the visual content can be used for instruction in applied music, serves to document a historically important music event, recreates the performance conditions of the period in which a work was composed, etc. Ethnomusicological video recordings are selected where the visual content is necessary for a full understanding of the context in which the music is performed. Documentaries on musical topics will be selected only if they will be used for classroom instruction. Dance and ballet recordings will be selected first based on the musical content and then secondarily for choreography and performance.

13. Computer Software

In general, current versions of computer software related to music are collected for Macintosh and IBM computers (in that order of preference). The library may collect databases of printed text, graphics, audio sounds, or instructional programs that do not require the student to produce sounds.

Software used for producing musical sounds (e.g., MIDI) and music writing are not collected. Software that accompanies materials in other formats will be retained in the collection regardless of which system is required to run it if the primary item can be used independently of the software. Where the primary item is dependent upon the use of the software, the selector will evaluate the currency of the system required to operate the software and consider the possibility of reformatting in cases of system obsolescence.

The acquisition of computer software for the music library's computer lab is not properly considered part of the library's collection. Acquisition of system software, word processing programs, spread sheets, music instructional programs, and other such programs requiring multiple simultaneous users or network access is not within the province of the Music Library's collection development program.

14. Electronic Formats

a. CD-ROM

It is still too early to evaluate exactly how CD-ROM technology will be used at Middlebury College. However, as greater experience is gained, more definite criteria for selection will be developed. Currently, CD-ROMs related to music that can be used in conjunction with Macintosh computers may be selected for the collection. CD-ROM products exceeding $100 will only be purchased if extensive use is anticipated for a particular course offering.

In the case of serial subscriptions to indexes and abstracts on CD-ROM in the field of music, the Starr Library Collection Development Policy (section V.C.) will be followed.

b. Internet Resources, Electronic Journals, etc.

This is another area which is just emerging. Collection policy will develop more definite criteria with experience. Currently, specific resources in music will be recommended to be included in the college's "gopher" that meet general interest (e.g., lyrics database, lists of music Internet resources) or are specifically requested by the faculty to support class instruction.

B. Special Collections
1. Music Student Theses

The Music Department will deposit one copy of all student theses prepared under their sponsorship. Copies of honors theses will be forwarded to Special Collections in Starr Library.

2. College Archival Materials

The papers and documents of the Music Department and Concert Series are retained by the College Archives in Starr Library. Recordings of local concerts are added to the Music Library.

3. Vermont Composers Consortium

The papers, documents, and selected works by members of this organization are deposited in the Music Library.

C. Languages and Translations

All books acquired for the collection are in English or in the original language with a parallel or accompanying translation. The following exceptions may be made: complete collections of correspondence by major composers may be acquired in the original language; major reference works (such as comprehensive music dictionaries, biographical dictionaries, and encyclopedias) in each of the major European languages (French, German, Italian, Russian, and Spanish); significant bibliographical studies; and works acquired for the summer language program. All periodicals will also be in English, but one major musicological journal in French, German, and Italian will also be acquired.

Printed music of vocal works not in English are acquired in the original language with an English translation whenever possible. Other translations of such works are acquired only if the work is well known in that translation.

Audio and video recordings of vocal music in the original language will be acquired unless the work is well known in a translation. Sound recordings of vocal music not in English should have an accompanying libretto with the original language and the English translation whenever possible. Video recordings of vocal works not in English should be subtitled in English whenever possible.

D. Local Publications and Works

The library acquires publications and recordings by the professors and applied music faculty currently teaching in the department. The library also collects manuscripts, manuscript facsimiles, and recordings of performances of musical works by composers currently teaching in the department.

The library selectively collects books, printed music, and recordings of well-known Vermont musicians.

E. Popular versus Scholarly Works

Books that are well-researched and written are collected. The library selectively collects books written for the mainstream classical music lover or opera buff. Books about popular music singers, instrumentalists, and groups, or opera stars and major conductors should give a well-researched and balanced treatment of the subject, neither excessively praising or denigrating. Such books are usually documented by footnotes, bibliography, and/or an index.

Current popular audio and video recordings are collected to historically document popular culture primarily in the United States and to a lesser degree in other parts of the world. Selection for this part of the collection will be based on a work's popularity with the population at large rather than on artistic or aesthetic criteria.

Since Middlebury College is not a research institution, the materials acquired are intended primarily for undergraduate students ages eighteen to twenty-one. Abstruse scholarly works intended for specialists are acquired very selectively to meet a specific instructional need.

F. Multiple Copies

It is standard policy to purchase only one copy of an item selected. However, not more than three copies of any one title are purchased to meet the demands of instruction. Multiple copies of the textbook used for a course are not collected. (See section G for the policy on multiple copies for reserve.)

Titles are not duplicated between various branches or collections of the Middlebury College Libraries except where a clear demand or need can be demonstrated.

G. Reserve Material

Reserve materials form a temporary subset of the library's collection and may be gathered from a variety of sources consisting of: books from the circulation collections of the Middlebury College Libraries; instructor's personal copies of any type of library material; reprints; pamphlets; audio and video recordings; software; and photocopies, dubs of sound recordings, and dubs of video recordings meeting the copyright compliance guidelines. The following materials may not be placed on reserve: materials received through interlibrary loan, reference books and scores, periodicals, any duplicated material that does not fully meet the copyright guidelines.

Personal copies are only placed and maintained on reserve if an item cannot be obtained by the time it is needed for instruction or if the item is unavailable for purchase. Personal copies will be removed from reserve when the library copy arrives. In general, no more than one copy will be purchased per fifteen students enrolled in any one class.

H. Reference Works
   1. General Principles
      The works in this collection are selected to meet the following objectives.

     a.    The collection will contain the most current, authoritative sources in the field.

     b.    Materials will be placed in the collection to insure equal and fair access to reference works for all users of the library.

     c.    The collection will emphasize materials which are frequently consulted by users and library staff.

     d.    The collection will contain a broad, general selection of materials in music emphasizing the needs and interests of an undergraduate college population.

Due to the space limitations of the reference area, the collection will not exceed the 108 linear feet allotted. However, this does not preclude the acquisition of reference materials that may be placed in the stacks and designated for library use only, but it does emphasize that materials marked as reference are the most frequently consulted reference materials.

The library has some basic general reference needs unrelated to music and will have: a current major general encyclopedia, the latest edition of an unabridged

American-English dictionary, foreign language dictionaries for each language taught at the college, at least one version of the Bible, various style manuals, and a current world atlas.

2. Specific Types of Materials about Music
   a. Directories, Yearbooks, and Almanacs
   The collection will contain the most current edition for works published in North America and Europe. Older editions will be withdrawn from the collection.

   b. Song Translations
   Major collections of art-song translations, both poetic and literal, will be maintained in reference.

   c. Quotations and Lists
   The collection contains books of quotations about music, lists of the names of musical pieces, and subject guides to vocal and instrumental music.

   d. Dictionaries and Encyclopedias
   The most current edition of the major encyclopedia or dictionary in music in each of the languages taught by the college is retained in reference. The most current edition of single volume dictionaries and encyclopedias with imprints less than fifty years ago will also be retained in reference. Older editions of all dictionaries and encyclopedias will be placed in the circulating collection. The second most current edition of single volume dictionaries will be rotated to Starr Library reference. Current editions of dictionaries of musical terms and biographical dictionaries in the languages taught by the college are in reference. Earlier editions are retained in the circulating collection and may also be rotated to

Starr Library in certain cases as requested by the Reference Department.

e. Music Publishing and Printing

Listings and catalogs of music publishers are kept in reference. The latest major publications on the legal and business aspects of music publishing and the recording industry will also be in reference.

f. Bibliographies

Bibliographies of music reference works, bibliographies, discographies, and periodicals; repertory lists for instrumental and vocal music; discographies of current popular music and lists of popular music charts; current evaluative discographies; and bibliographies covering broad areas of music literature are in reference. Bibliographies on specialized topics and for individual musicians are shelved in the circulating collection.

g. Indexes

Indexes to general periodical literature or of a general nature are in reference. Indexes to specific periodicals are shelved with the corresponding periodical.

h. Thematic Catalogs

The most current thematic catalogs or lists of the works of individual composers are in reference. Bibliographies for individual composers are retained in reference if they contain the only current complete listing of the composer's works.

i. Chronologies

The latest editions of chronologies of music are kept in reference.

j. Histories of Music
The latest editions of multivolume histories of music reflecting current musicological scholarship are shelved in reference.

3. Evaluation and Inventory
The reference collection will undergo an inventory and evaluation at least every two years. Each work will be examined to see if it meets the above criteria.

I. Government Publications
Government publications about music that are part of the materials acquired through the depository system are acquired by the Music Library.

J. Acquisitions Procedures Affecting Collections Policies
1. Standing Orders
Standing orders for sets, series, and recording labels are established to ensure that materials of known value to the library's collection development policy are acquired expeditiously and in their entirety. This is particularly important where gaps in a set would diminish the value of the set as a whole. Standing orders will not be established unless it is anticipated that the library would acquire at least 80 percent of the titles to be ordered. Standing orders should not exceed 50 percent of any one budget line in order to preserve adequate funding for firm orders to support immediate curricular needs.

Standing orders for recording labels and series will be placed for labels and series that cover a well-defined subject area (e.g., early music, computer music, ethnomusicological recordings, contemporary music) where comprehensiveness is desirable and to expedite the receipt of materials.

2. Approval Plans and Blanket Orders
   a. Books
      Approval plans for university press publications are maintained.

   b. Scores
      See Appendix 1 for approval plan for scores.

3. Gifts and Exchanges.
   The Music Library follows the Middlebury College Library Gifts Policy Statement.

K. Expensive Purchases
   Items exceeding $500 in cost will receive greater scrutiny. Consultation will be done with other persons, including the collection development librarian, college librarian, music faculty, or other persons who may be involved in the selection of the item. These discussions may include the appropriateness of the selection, special funding arrangements, and/or placement in a special collection.

# Appendix: Obtaining Copies of Policies

The chair of the Resource Sharing and Collection Development Committee, Music Library Association, regularly solicits copies of collection development policies for music from all types of libraries and will make available a copy of a policy on request. The annual Music Library Association *Membership Handbook* provides an updated list of the chairs and members of all Music Library Association committees every year.[31]

In addition, libraries are increasingly making their collection policies available on the World Wide Web. A search using one of the standard Web searching tools for terms such as "music collection policies" yields several music collection development policies available for perusal on the Web.

# Glossary[32]

*ANSCR. Alpha-Numeric System for Classification of Recordings* (see n. 24).

**approval plan.** Arrangement between a library and a publisher or dealer in which the library receives current books, scores, or recordings in specified subjects. The materials are selected by the publisher or dealer and returns are generally permitted.

**archival boxing.** Inexpensive boxes custom built by library binders to preserve worn, damaged, or loose materials that cannot otherwise be bound. Also called phase boxes.

**arrangement.** Reworking or adaptation of a musical work for a medium of performance different from its original medium.

**charts.** Record-rating lists that rank recordings according to sales or radio exposure; also, written arrangements of jazz or pop tunes.

**chorus score.** Score showing only the chorus parts of a vocal work; the accompaniment, if any, is arranged for a keyboard instrument. *See also* Vocal score.

**classical music.** See Western art music.

**close score.** Score showing all the parts on a minimum number of staves, usually two, as with hymns.

**collected works.** *See* complete works.

**collecting levels** or **collection levels.** Codes or descriptors used in collection assessment and development to describe collection strengths and collecting intensities.

**collection development.** The process of planning, building, and maintaining a library's information resources.

**collection management.** Ensuring effective collection development through methods such as collection analysis and evaluation; collection review for decisions about preservation, remote storage, protected access, and deselection; use and user studies; and vendor and dealer assessments.

**complete works.** Critical edition of a composer's works, usually issued in a series, that attempts to be complete and authentic. Such editions are used primarily for research and do not usually include performance parts.

**condensed score.** Score showing only the principal parts on a minimum number of staves, and generally organized by instrumental sections.

**conspectus.** An overview or summary of collection strengths and collecting intensities, arranged by subject, classification scheme, or a combination of either, and containing standardized codes for collection or collecting levels and for languages of materials collected.

**cylinder recording.** Hollow cylinder with sound recorded on the grooved outer surface; one of the earliest types of sound recording, popular from the 1890s through the 1920s.

**deselection.** Periodic withdrawal of library materials according to collection management guidelines.

**document delivery.** Transmission of library materials electronically or by courier, mail, or fax.

**dub.** A copy of a previously made recording.

**DVD.** Digital Video Disc (also called Digital Versatile Disc) recording, 4 3/4 inches in diameter.

**early music.** Term used mainly since the 1960s to refer to music from the Middle Ages and the Renaissance (up to 1600), sometimes also to the Baroque period (up to 1750), and more recently to music of the Classical period (up to 1800) as well.

**ethnic music.** Any music (classical, folk, popular, religious, etc.) that belongs to an ethnic group. Ethnic subdivisions are usually linguistic or national but can be broader or smaller, such as ethnic classical music of North India, which comprises several languages but does not include South India.

**fakebooks.** Bound collections of sheet music showing the melody and chord progressions (chord symbols or guitar tablature), and sometimes lyrics, of jazz or popular tunes.

**fanzine.** Magazine written by and for avid supporters ("fans") of a particular performer, usually written without official approval.

**folk music.** Music of any linguistic group that is not art or popular music, and usually not religious, and not requiring professional training to perform. Often associated with rural cultures and disseminated through oral transmission.

**full score.** Score showing all the instrumental and vocal parts on separate staves in vertical alignment, so that the parts can be read simultaneously.

**iconography.** The analysis and interpretation of musical subject matter in works of art.

**instantaneous disc recording.** A recording made directly onto disc or magnetic tape during performance, playable immediately afterward, and generally existing as a unique copy.

**instrumental method.** Instructional guide to learning the technique for playing a specific instrument, usually including studies and exercises.

**laser disc.** Digital video recording on twelve-inch disc.

**libretto.** The literary text of an extended vocal work such as an opera, oratorio, or musical comedy.

**miniature score.** Full score whose music notation and text are reduced in size; intended for study rather than for performance.

**monumental edition.** A multivolume collection of works by a number of composers, illustrating the musical style of a given period, an aspect of the history of music, or representative music of a national group.

**multimedia products.** Interactive computer files, often in CD-ROM format, that utilize sound, text, and images.

**NTSC.** National Television Standards Committee, responsible for setting television and video broadcast standards in the United States.

**octavo.** In music publishing, a choral score; originally named after its octavo format, a folio sheet folded three times.

**open reel.** A tape wound on an unenclosed reel and requiring a separate unenclosed take-up reel during playback.

**organology.** The study of musical instruments, their historical development, and musical uses.

**PAL.** Phase Alternate Line: a color television broadcast system used in the United Kingdom and many other countries.

**part.** Printed music showing the music for only one performer in an ensemble and intended for use in performance.

**performance practice.** As applied to Western music, the term involves all aspects of the way in which music is and has been performed, including interpretation of notation, improvisation and ornaments, choice of instruments, voice production, tuning, pitch, and temperament.

**piano score.** A reduction of an orchestral score to a version for piano, on two staves.

**piano-vocal score.** *See* vocal score.

**pop-folio** or **popular music folio.** Scores comprised of transcriptions of sound recordings and usually arranged for voice and piano with guitar chord diagrams and chord symbols.

**popular music.** Mass-marketed, composed music accessible to and enjoyed by the general public, as distinguished from art music intended for musically educated listeners.

**reduction.** Arrangement, usually for piano, of an orchestral work.

**reissue.** A second or repeated issue of a sound recording. Also called a rerelease.

**remote storage.** Off-site housing of library materials.

**SECAM.** Sequential Couleur avec Memoire, or Sequential Color with Memory: a color television broadcast system used by a few countries, including France and Russia.

**set.** A group of volumes that forms a complete publication on a particular subject; e.g., collected works of a composer.

**sheet music.** Music printed on unbound sheets of paper.

**standard repertory.** Musical works from the Baroque period through the twentieth century that are performed on a regular basis.

**standing order.** Formal arrangement with a publisher or vendor to send all of the publications in a series or set as they are issued.

**study score.** *See* miniature score.

**transcription.** Arrangement of music for a medium of performance different from its original medium; also, the notation of live or recorded music on staff paper.

**urtext.** Edition of a musical work ("text") that attempts to show the work as the composer originally intended, without editorial additions or changes.

**vernacular music.** In cultures with an art music tradition, this term designates more "common" music, which can be folk, religious, or popular.

**vertical files.** Collections of pamphlets, clippings, and similar materials arranged in file folders for ready reference in a drawer, box, or suitable case.

**VHS.** Videocassette recording format.

**vocal score.** Score of a vocal work showing all vocal parts; the accompaniment, if any, is arranged for keyboard instrument. *See also* chorus score.

**Western art music** or **"classical" music.** Concert music from the era of Western liturgical chant up to the present, usually composed and notated, and requiring professional training to perform and some musical education to appreciate.

**world music.** An umbrella term used to designate ethnic musics of all types, usually excluding European art music. Although the recording industry excludes jazz and rock when using this term, it applies this label to modern fusion music, which blends music from many traditions, sometimes including jazz or rock.

# Notes

1. Joanne S. Anderson et al., *Guide for Written Collection Policy Statements*, 2d ed., Collection Management and Development Guides, no. 7 (Chicago: American Library Association, 1996).

2. Ibid., 27–28.

3. Ibid., 28.

4. Ibid., 3.

5. Dan C. Hazen, "Collection Development Policies in the Information Age," *College & Research Libraries* 56 (January 1995): 29–30.

6. Richard Snow, "Wasted Words: The Written Collection Development Policy and the Academic Library," *Journal of Academic Librarianship* 22 (May 1996): 192–93.

7. Ibid., 193.

8. Anderson et al., 2.

9. Hazen, 31.

10. Anderson et al., 3.

11. Ibid., 1–3.

12. Collection Development Policies Committee, Collection Development and Evaluation Section, RASD, "The Relevance of Collection Development Policies: Definition, Necessity, and Applications," *RQ* 33 (fall 1993): 66.

13. Adapted from Anderson et al., 6–7.

14. Anderson et al., 1–3.

15. Kay Ann Cassell and Elizabeth Futas, *Developing Public Library Collections, Policies, and Procedures: A How-to-Do-It Manual for Small and Medium-Sized Public Libraries* (New York: Neal-Schuman, 1991), 63–85.

16. Barbara Lockett, ed., *Guide to the Evaluation of Library Collections*, Collection Management and Development Guides, no. 2 (Chicago: American Library Association, 1989); Lenore Clark, ed., *Guide to Review of Library Collections: Preservation, Storage, and Withdrawal*, Collection Management and Development Guides, no. 5 (Chicago: American Library Association, 1991).

17. Gordon Rowley, *Organization of Collection Development*, SPEC Kit 207 (Washington, D.C.: Association of Research Libraries, Office of Management Services, 1995), 149–73.

18. Michael A. Keller, "Music," in *Selection of Library Materials in the Humanities, Social Sciences, and Sciences*, ed. Patricia A. McClung (Chicago: American Library Association, 1985), 139–63.

19. Elizabeth Davis, coord. ed., Pamela Bristah and Jane Gottlieb, scores eds., Kent Underwood and William E. Anderson, sound recordings eds., *A Basic Music Library: Essential Scores and Sound Recordings*, 3rd ed. (Chicago: American Library Association, 1997), 567–76; Elizabeth Davis, "Guidelines for Evaluating Music Collections as Part of a Regional Assessment Plan," in *Collection Assessment in Music Libraries*, ed. Jane Gottlieb, MLA Technical Reports, no. 22 (Canton, Mass.: Music Library Association, 1994), 38–49.

20. Anderson et al., 8–10.

21. Ibid., 28.

22. Jane Gottlieb, "Introduction: Collection Assessment in Music Libraries," in *Collection Assessment in Music Libraries*, ed. Jane Gottlieb, MLA Technical Reports, no. 22 (Canton, Mass.: Music Library Association, 1994), 1–6; Peggy Daub, "The RLG Music Conspectus: Its History and Applications," in *Collection Assessment in Music Libraries*, 7–24; Davis, "Guidelines," 25–49.

23. "Appendix: The RLG Music Conspectus Lines," *Collection Assessment in Music Libraries*, 82–88.

24. George Sherman Dickinson, *Classification of Musical Compositions: A Decimal-Symbol System* (Poughkeepsie, N.Y.: Vassar College, 1938); Caroline Saheb-Ettaba and Roger B. McFarland, *ANSCR: The Alpha-Numeric System for Classification of Recordings* (Williamsport, Pa.: Bro-Dart, 1969); Melvil Dewey, *Dewey Decimal Classification and Relative Index*, 21st ed. by Joan S. Mitchell, Julianne Beall, Winton E. Matthews Jr. and Gregory R. New (Albany, N.Y.: Forest Press, 1996).

25. Mona L. Scott, *Conversion Tables: LC-Dewey, Dewey-LC* (Englewood, Colo.: Libraries Unlimited, 1993).

26. Anderson et al., 9, 11.

27. Lenore Coral, "Evaluating the Conspectus Approach: Problems and Alternatives," in *Collection Assessment in Music Libraries*, 76–79.

28. Anderson et al., 9–10.

29. These codes for music are listed by Peggy Daub on p. 10 in *Collection Assessment in Music Libraries*.

30. These categories are listed on pp. 84–87 in "Appendix: The RLG Music Conspectus Lines," in *Collection Assessment in Music Libraries*.

31. Music Library Association, *Membership Handbook* (Canton, Mass.: Music Library Association, 1993– ).

32. These definitions are adapted from several sources, most particularly from Anderson et al.; *Anglo-American Cataloguing Rules*, 2d ed., 1988 rev. (Chicago: American Library Association, 1988), 615–24; and Suzanne E. Thorin and Carole Franklin Vidali, *The Acquisition and Cataloging of Music and Sound Recordings: A Glossary*, MLA Technical Reports, no. 11 ([Canton, Mass.]: Music Library Association, 1984).

# Selected Bibliography

## WRITING COLLECTION POLICIES

Anderson, Joanne S., et al. *Guide for Written Collection Policy Statements.* 2d ed. Collection Management and Development Guides, no. 7. Chicago: American Library Association, 1996.

Cassell, Kay Ann, and Elizabeth Futas. *Developing Public Library Collections, Policies, and Procedures: A How-to-Do-It Manual for Small and Medium-Sized Public Libraries.* New York: Neal-Schuman, 1991.

Clark, Lenore, ed. *Guide to Review of Library Collections: Preservation, Storage, and Withdrawal.* Collection Management and Development Guides, no. 5. Chicago: American Library Association, 1991.

Collection Development Policies Committee. Collection Development and Evaluation Section. RASD. "The Relevance of Collection Development Policies: Definition, Necessity, and Applications." *RQ* 33 (fall 1993): 65–74.

Coscarelli, William F., and Anna H. Perrault. "Music Collections in ARL Libraries: A Report of a Survey at Louisiana State University." *Collection Management* 16, no. 2 (1992): 13–59.

Futas, Elizabeth, ed. *Collection Development Policies and Procedures.* 3rd ed. Phoenix, Ariz.: Oryx Press, 1995.

Hazen, Dan C. "Collection Development Policies in the Information Age." *College & Research Libraries* 56 (January 1995): 29–31.

Lein, Edward. "Suggestions for Formulating Collection Development Policy Statements for Music Score Collections in Academic Libraries." *Collection Management* 9 (winter 1987): 69–101.

Lockett, Barbara, ed. *Guide to the Evaluation of Library Collections.* Collection Management and Development Guides, no. 2. Chicago: American Library Association, 1989.

*Reference Collection Development: A Manual.* RASD Occasional Papers, no. 13. Chicago: Reference and Adult Services Division, American Library Association, 1992.

Rowley, Gordon. *Organization of Collection Development.* SPEC Kit 207. Washington, D.C.: Association of Research Libraries, Office of Management Services, 1995.

Snow, Richard. "Wasted Words: The Written Collection Development Policy and the Academic Library." *Journal of Academic Librarianship* 22 (May 1996): 191–94.

## MUSIC COLLECTIONS:
## DEVELOPMENT AND ASSESSMENT

The list below consists primarily of periodical articles and monograph chapters. It is not intended to be comprehensive, and readers are encouraged to survey the professional literature regularly for similar and more recent writings. The discussion under "Selection tools" on pages 11–12 offers suggestions for finding many selection and assessment tools not listed here. Readers are advised especially to consult books comprised of bibliographies, discographies, and histories devoted to particular types of music, which are beyond the scope of the list below.

Annichiarico, Mark, Rod Bustos, Thomas N. Jewell, Adam Mazmanian, and Bill Piekarski. "And the Beat Goes On." *Library Journal* 120 (15 November 1995): 32–36.

Connolly, Bruce. "Popular Music on Compact Disc: A 'First-Purchase' Discography." *Library Journal* 110 (15 November 1985): 42–48.

Cooper, B. Lee. "An Opening Day Collection of Popular Music Resources: Searching for Discographic Standards." In *Twentieth-Century Popular Culture in Museums and Libraries*, ed. Fred E. H. Schroeder, 226–55. Bowling Green, Ohio: Bowling Green University Popular Press, 1981.

Cross, Nigel. "A Survey of Fanzines." *Brio* 18 (autumn/winter 1981): 1–18.

Davis, Elizabeth. "Guidelines for Evaluating Music Collections as Part of a Regional Assessment Plan." In *Collection Assessment in Music Libraries*, edited by Jane Gottlieb, 25–49. MLA Technical Reports, no. 22. Canton, Mass.: Music Library Association, 1994.

Davis, Elizabeth, coord. ed., Pamela Bristah and Jane Gottlieb, scores eds., Kent Underwood and William E. Anderson, sound recordings eds. *A Basic Music Library: Essential Scores and Sound Recordings*. 3rd ed. Chicago: American Library Association, 1997.

De Lerma, Dominique-René. "The Undergraduate and His Music." *Choice* 8 (November 1971): 1146–50.

Farrington, James. "Putting Dastgah-ha, Didjeridus, and the Diga Rhythm Band in the Library: Collecting World Music." In *World Music in Music Libraries*, edited by Carl Rahkonen, 26–40. MLA Technical Reports, no. 24. Canton, Mass: Music Library Association, 1994.

Fedunok, Suzanne. "Hammurabi and the Electronic Age: Documenting Electronic Collection Decisions." *RQ* 36 (Fall 1996): 86–90.

Ginsburg, David D. "Rock Is a Way of Life: The World of Rock-n-Roll Fanzines and Fandom." *Serials Review* 5 (January–March 1979): 29–46.

Griffin, Marie P. "Jazz: An Afro-American Art Music." *Drexel Library Quarterly* 19 (winter 1983): 55–77.

Hendricks, Leta. "Getting Hip to the Hop: A Rap Bibliography/Discography." *Music Reference Services Quarterly* 4, no. 4 (1996): 17–57.

Hoffmann, Frank W. "Popular Music Periodicals in the Library." *Serials Librarian* 12, no. 3/4 (1987): 69–88.

Jaffe, Lee David. "The Last Days of the Avant Garde; Or How to Tell Your Glass from Your Eno." *Drexel Library Quarterly* 19 (winter 1983): 105–22.

Keller, Michael A. "Music." In *Selection of Library Materials in the Humanities, Social Sciences, and Sciences*, edited by Patricia A. McClung, 139–63. Chicago: American Library Association, 1985.

Krummel, D. W. "Musical Editions: A Basic Collection." *Choice* 13 (April 1976): 177–95.

Murray, James Briggs. "Understanding and Developing Black Popular Music Collections." *Drexel Library Quarterly* 19 (winter 1983): 4–54.

Politis, John. "Rock Music's Place in the Library." *Drexel Library Quarterly* 19 (winter 1983): 78–92.

Pressler, Charles A. "Rock and Roll: Dimensions of a Cultural Revolution." *Choice* 29 (April 1992): 1192–201.

Rebman, Elisabeth. "Music." In *The Humanities and the Library*. 2d ed., edited by Nena Couch and Nancy Allen, 132–72. Chicago: American Library Association, 1993.

Schurk, William L. "Uncovering the Mysteries of Popular Recordings Collection Development." *The Acquisitions Librarian*, no. 8 (1992): 91–98. Also published in *Popular Culture and Acquisitions*, ed. Allen Ellis (New York: Haworth Press, 1992).

Sparkman, Kathleen. "Moving Your Country Collection into the Mainstream." *Library Journal* 121 (1 November 1996): 39–42.

Swisher, Christopher C. "The Folk Music Revival on Record." *Drexel Library Quarterly* 19 (winter 1983): 93–104.

Tarakan, Sheldon Lewis. "Classical Pop: Documenting Popular Musical Culture in Library Audio Collections." *Drexel Library Quarterly* 19 (winter 1983): 123–50.

Theil, Gordon. "Popular Music Sound Recordings: Recommendations on Selection, Arrangement and Cataloging." *Phonographic Bulletin* 38 (March 1984): 29–33.

# Index

# About the Authors

Amanda Maple is music librarian and head of the Arts and Humanities Library at the Pennsylvania State University. She has written articles about various aspects of music librarianship and served as assistant editor of the Music Library Association's journal, *Notes*.

Jean Morrow is director of libraries at the New England Conservatory of Music and teaches music librarianship at Simmons Graduate School of Library and Information Science. She is editor of the Music Library Association's *Basic Manual Series*.